ALAN RIACH is the Professor of Scottish Literature at Glasgow University and currently the President of the Association for Scottish Literary Studies. He is the general editor of the *Collected Works* of Hugh MacDiarmid (Carcanet), the author of *Representing Scotland in Literature, Popular Culture and Iconography* (Palgrave Macmillan, 2005) and co-author with Alexander Moffat of *Arts of Resistance: Poets, Portraits and Landscapes of Modern Scotland* (Luath Press, 2008), described by the *Times Literary Supplement* as 'a landmark book'. His fourth book of poems, *Clearances* (2001), follows *First & Last Songs* (1995), *An Open Return* (1991) and *This Folding Map* (1990). His radio series *The Good of the Arts* was first broadcast in New Zealand in 2001 and repeated a number of times on Radio New Zealand's Concert Programme. Born in Airdrie, Lanarkshire, Scotland, in 1957, he went to school in England, in Gravesend, Kent, and completed his first degree in English Literature at Cambridge University and his PhD in Scottish Literature at Glasgow University, before working at the University of Waikato in New Zealand, 1986–2000. Since 1 January 2001, he has been living in Scotland.

Other books by Alan Riach

Poetry

This Folding Map
An Open Return
First & Last Songs
Clearances

Criticism

Hugh MacDiarmid's Epic Poetry
The Poetry of Hugh MacDiarmid
*Representing Scotland in Literature, Iconography and Popular
  Culture: The Masks of the Modern Nation*
with Alexander Moffat, *Arts of Resistance: Poets, Portraits and
  Landscapes of Modern Scotland*

As General Editor

The Collected Works of Hugh MacDiarmid

As Co-Editor

The Radical Imagination: Lectures and Talks by Wilson Harris
Scotlands: Poets and the Nation
*The Edinburgh Companion to Twentieth-Century Scottish
  Literature*

Homecoming

New Poems 2001–2009

ALAN RIACH

Luath Press Limited
EDINBURGH
www.luath.co.uk

First published 2009

ISBN: 978-1-906817-09-1

The publishers acknowledge the support of

Scottish
Arts Council

towards the publication of this volume.

The paper used in this book is recyclable. It is made from
low chlorine pulps produced in a low energy, low emission manner
from renewable forests.

Printed and bound by
Bell & Bain Ltd., Glasgow

Typeset in 10.5 point Sabon by
3btype.com

for Edwin Morgan, *maestro*

Contents

CONTENTS

Acknowledgements

SOME OF THESE POEMS, or earlier versions of them, have appeared in the following books, anthologies, journals and newspapers and I am very grateful to their editors: *The Listener* (New Zealand); *The University of Waikato Alumni Magazine* (New Zealand); *Chapman*; *The Dark Horse*; *In Scotland*; *Markings*; *Poetry Scotland*; *daemon* 7 & 8: 60/60; *The Brownsbank Broadsheet*; *Southlight*; *The Avenue* (Glasgow University Magazine); *The Herald*; *die horen – Zeitschrift für Literatur, Kunst und Kritik* (Germany); *Anglo-Files* (Denmark); *Quadrant* (Australia); CHOMBEC *News* (Centre for the History of Music in Britain, the Empire and the Commonwealth, University of Bristol); *Archipelago* (Oxford); *Without Day: proposals for a new Scottish parliament*, edited by Alec Finlay (Edinburgh: Pocket Books, 2000); *Scotlands: Poets and the Nation*, edited by Douglas Gifford and Alan Riach (Manchester: Carcanet Press and Edinburgh: Scottish Poetry Library, 2004); *Spirits of the Age: Scottish Self Portraits*, edited by Paul Henderson Scott (Edinburgh: The Saltire Society, 2005); *The Wallace Muse: Poems and artworks inspired by the life and legend of William Wallace*, edited by Lesley Duncan and Elspeth King (Edinburgh: Luath Press, 2005); *A Door Open to the World: Poetry Collection of the 1st Qinghai Lake International Poetry Festival* (China: Qinghai Provincial Government, 2007); 'The Boy and the Horse' was published in Chinese translation in *The Entrance of the Last Pure Land* (China, Xining City: Qinghai People's Publishing, 2009); *New Writing Scotland 25: The Dyamics of Balsa* and *New Writing Scotland 26: Bucket of Frogs* both edited by Liz Niven and Brian Whittingham (Glasgow: Association for Scottish Literary Studies, 2007 and 2008, respectively); *David Daiches: A Celebration of His Life and Work*, edited by Willam Baker and Michael Lister (Brighton, England and Portland, USA: Sussex Academic Press, 2008); *Stepping Westward: Inaugural Lectures* by Nigel Leask and Alan Riach (Glasgow: Association for Scottish Literary Studies and the University of Glasgow, 2008); *Arts of Resistance: Poets, Portraits and Landscapes of Modern Scotland* by Alexander Moffat and Alan Riach, with contributions from Linda MacDonald-Lewis (Edinburgh: Luath Press, 2008); *For Angus: A Book for Angus Calder. Poems, Prose, Sketches and Music*, ed. Richard Berengarten and Gideon Calder (Cambridge: Los Poetry Press, 2009); *Adrian: Scotland Celebrates Adrian Mitchell*, ed. Chrys Salt and John Hudson (Gatehouse of Fleet: Markings Publications, 2009).

'The Confrontation' is largely, but not entirely, transcribed from Bryan Gilliam, *The Life of Richard Strauss* (Cambridge University Press, 1999), and is published with the kind approval of Bryan Gilliam. As well as various biographies of the composer, including Michael Kennedy, *Portrait of Elgar* (London: Oxford University Press, 1968), Basil Maine, *Elgar: His Life and Works* (London: G. Bell & Sons, Ltd., 1933), and W. H. Reed, *Elgar* (London: J. M. Dent, 1939), 'Elgar in Scotland' draws on the article of the same name by Geoffrey Elgar (pen-name of Peter G. Elgar), in *History Scotland*, vol.6, no.6 (November/December 2006), pp.40–43, and is published with the kind approval of Mr Elgar.

'February Morning: Traffic' in 2003, and 'Mahler 10: Adagio', 'The Dogs of Scotland', 'Bus Stop: Alloway, Spring' and 'Lanarkshire, January' in 2004, were published as limited edition 'Poet-Books' with paintings by Chan Ky-Yut.

The China Memorandum was completed as a result of an invitation to travel and write in the Guangxi Province in November/December 2004, with artists and poets from China and Australia, made by Alexander Moffat, then Head of Painting at Glasgow School of Art; the resulting poems (translated into Chinese) and art works were mounted as exhibitions at the Guangxi Arts Institute and then at the Central Academy of Fine Arts in Beijing in 2004. I am especially grateful to Sandy Moffat for the illustrations accompanying the poems in this sequence and also for the final illustrations in the book, for 'The Bridge to Dunskiath'. These are from 'The Dunskiath Suite' which Sandy completed at the suggestion of the poet and editor Andrew McNeillie and were first published in his journal *Archipelago*, so my thanks also go to Andrew for unobtrusively initiating good work from behind the scenes.

I am very grateful to Michael Clark for permission to reproduce the image of his painting, 'Ayrshire Skies' on the cover of this book. His website address is: www.michaelclarkartist.co.uk

For checking the names of the different types of barbed wire noted in 'Bonanza', I am grateful to John Marquess of The Ponderosa, Glenshane Pass, Co. Derry, N. Ireland.

Edward Dorn's poem, 'The Protestant View' is printed as an epigraph to *The China Memorandum* with the kind permission of Jennifer Dunbar Dorn.

For comments on drafts of some of the poems, I would like to thank Edwin Morgan, Les Murray, Lesley Duncan, Joy Hendry and Liz Lochhead. And extra gratitude to Liz for her characteristically generous preface.

Thanks overall to Leila Cruickshank, Senga and Anne Fairgrieve, Tom Bee and Gavin MacDougall at Luath Press: the product is the proof.

It is the simplest but the deepest thanks I would offer to my wife Rae, especially for her love through the years in which these poems were written, in a home that was still very much in the making for her. I travelled single to New Zealand in 1986. I returned a married man with two young boys. There is an obvious point too easy to pass over that should have pause and acknowledgement, with regard to the poems: one begins writing for oneself, and then with a sense of readers beyond oneself. I'm still just young enough to remember when I knew all of my readers personally. If you're lucky enough to get older, though, your daily life is filled with other people, other things. So, most closely, thanks to Rae, and to James and David, for the unique qualifications they have given me, and just for being who they are.

Preface

THIS COLLECTION ABOUNDS in images of arcs, arches, bridges, of the great curving transits round the orb of the world modern life affords us, of borders crossed, shadow-lines traversed, connections made. Things go flying – books, in an impulse of the imagination, like the compulsively squandered coins of childhood, into the sea; the rat that Glen kills; the improbably athletic grandfather in 'The Memory'; diverse and various voyagers; the singular poetic persona its very self – all are flung far, in great, airy, liberating trajectories. Again and again the poet delights in 'the unpredicted'.

This word 'unpredicted' keeps coming up, in poem after poem, and for Riach, this is never a source of dread, but always a positive, if not necessarily by any means an easy thing. It is 'the unpredicted' that seems to be the prime source of his poetic muse. The arc of that long journey out and away is always, conversely and finally, towards home.

This collection, more than most, benefits by being read in sequence. It starts, spare, on the furthest shores of New Zealand and after a sequence in China touches on, expands upon, so many other places – Istanbul; Chambésy near Lake Léman; Helsinki; Mexico; the Wild West Badlands of Northern Ireland; Wales; the High Plains of a visit to Edward Dorn; and people – Herman Melville visits Glasgow; Pushkin is translated into Scotland and into Scots – but ends in the last section: *Right Here*. And we know that what is being celebrated is the rightness, for Riach, of being here. Now.

As Andrew McNellie has written of Alan Riach, 'Scotland is his agenda'.

And for me, it's the Scottish poems, the *Right Here* poems, which are, I must confess, my favourites, when they're at home. The heart and the core of the thing. A lyric like 'Bus Stop, Alloway: Spring' gladdens my heart as much as 'Drumelzier', with its eldritch conversation, draws me back, disturbed but quite convinced, again

5

and again. Riach is concerned with what lies underneath even as it is Scotland and its hard and brilliant adamantine surfaces that fire him – the North, where, as Elgar, in the dramatic monologue poem about him and his travels in Scotland, notes:

> the air indeed was different. Something happened.
> The space you could be lonely in was open.

Alan Riach is Professor in the Department of Scottish Literature at Glasgow University, which is a bit more than a day job. It would be impossible, for Riach at least, to do it without his whole self being steeped in the contemporary cultures, issues, identities and politics, as well as in the literature and history, of this country.

As an academic, his passion is for generous, accessible, illuminating criticism and research. Here too the drive is towards making connections, rejoicing in contradictions. The creativity of both his academic work and his poetry has, as its engine, the largesse of spirit necessary to embrace both contradiction and connection. And for Riach, though he is a very knowledgeable and involved commentator upon Scottish *painting* and the correspondences between the modern movements of the last century in both the literary and the fine art scenes – see the recent book *Arts of Resistance* which he co-authored with Alexander Moffat – nevertheless the purely creative side of him comes out not in personal experiments in the visual arts, nor in prose fiction, but in his poetry.

In 2009, the 250th anniversary of the birth of Robert Burns, the Scottish Government decided to declare 'The Year of Homecoming' as an international marketing slogan, hoping to persuade the multitude of people from all over the world who can trace their ancestry to Scotland to come back as tourists. But, for Riach, the word – way beyond the mass-advertising hype – clearly carries many, potent, multi-faceted meanings. Therefore the poems in this, his *Homecoming,* explore the complexities of these with love, curiosity, optimism and commitment.

It's great to have this new collection in print.

Liz Lochhead
May 2009

Homecoming: An Introduction

> Instinctively, I turn towards the window when the captain
> announces that we have entered the Nigerian air-space.
> WOLE SOYINKA, *You Must Set Forth at Dawn*

FIRST THERE IS THE setting out. Home is what you leave. From childhood's hour, the opening sentence of Stevenson's *Kidnapped* has haunted generations with its intuitive truth of departure, leave-taking, putting the home you come from behind you and setting forth like Odysseus, into the unforeseen:

> I will begin the story of my adventures with a certain
> morning early in the month of June, the year of grace 1751,
> when I took the key for the last time out of the door of my
> father's house.

We are then to be lured by our trust up the winding stairs of the ruined tower, learn to watch out for ourselves, where to place our feet on the unreliable stone; we are bound to be kidnapped by Uncles Ebenezer, Captains Hoseason, sold into adulthood, learn about resistance, who will help, where the inimical comes from, and how, despite all that seems set to prevent it, sometimes, leaping from a momentary meeting, an encounter you couldn't predict, will come friendship, someone to fight *beside*, and common cause. What follows is the chase, the long traverse of wandering through unfamiliar territories, and, if you're lucky, companionship. Friendship is at the heart of *Kidnapped*, but leavetaking is both its start, and ending: how to say farewell.

Loneliness is part of the story, but there are others as well, a deeper resource that arises when you find a way to return, to cautiously move back down the steps of the tower, to cross the world again, from west to east, returning to something you find you're obliged to renew. For home is a deal made with midnight, something signed, sealed and promised before you were born.

So you can go home, after all. A sense of belonging is something to value, for it always comes at a cost, and the pleasures and problems company brings are part of that, not least through that structure of human gathering that remains the source of all literary comedy and tragedy alike: the family.

I have always enjoyed the idea of homecoming. For many years, school ended with homecomings to look forward to, at lunch and then again at the end of the day. Lanarkshire was where I was born, and grandparents, uncles and aunts and cousins and friends remained there and in Glasgow while my mother's position as a schoolteacher of mathematics and my father's seafaring as Captain with the Merchant Navy came to an end and he took a post as a Trinity House Pilot, taking ships down the London river, and we moved to England, to Kent. So there were innumerable homecomings to Scotland, driving north over long days across landscapes to a border that never failed to be meaningful. Edwin Morgan's poem 'The Solway Canal' reminds me how marvellous it would be to build such a waterway in reality and see the pleasure crafts sailing along it. Sometimes we would arrive unannounced, enter by the back door, as it were, and seat ourselves by the coal fire for my grandparents to come in from the sitting room or kitchen and find us transported as if by magic to the ancestral hearth, with wonderment, delight and the marvellous conjuring of feasts of food and gatherings of people to ensue.

Such festivities were especially riotous at Hogmanay, on New Year's Eve. Every effort would go into the preparations and then nothing would happen till midnight, but every year, family would try to get together to be with my grandparents for the Bells. I remember one year arriving by train from England and getting the blue train out from Glasgow to Airdrie to be met by Uncle Alex and driven at top speed the two miles out to the village with seconds to spare before midnight. The gate of the year, everybody knew, was a moment where you paused, a threshold you stepped over gingerly. We all tried to get home each year in time to do that.

Later, there would be the many returns to my parents' house in Kent, where, over the university years of undergraduate study at Cambridge and postgraduate research at Glasgow, I had left two walls of my room covered with accumulated books and a desk stocked with papers and notes, poems that may or may not be worth preserving. And then in 1986, after a year of various jobs, driving and delivering around Glasgow and across Scotland, roof-surveying that let me climb to otherwise forbidden heights of the city, and unemployment that left me sometimes for periods of time economising to the point of serious frugality and pinch, and with no prospect of gainful employment in the Thatcher-era UK universities, I took up the offer of a post-doctoral research fellowship at the University of Waikato, Hamilton, New Zealand, and flew into the dark unknown. I literally knew no-one there and truly had no notion at that time of what I was going to. I left the poems I had written in a box under my desk, thinking, now I will find out if they are going to be required. If not, I would abandon that work forever.

At first there was the option of one or three years. I chose to go for one year. A long voyage, one of my father's seafaring colleagues told me. Fourteen years later, married now and with two boys, I returned to Scotland on New Year's Day, 2001. Happily, this would be as firm a declaration of homecoming as anyone could make. Even when the novelty wears off, I told my father, there will simply be the pleasures of walking around here. 'No,' he sternly replied. 'You are wrong. The novelty will *never* wear off.'

It was a much longer voyage than predicted and there were many homecomings. For a number of years, the rhythm of work became balanced and productive. Regularly, there would be expeditions into the depths of the National Library of Scotland, allowing me to draw up treasures and make away with boxes and files of photocopied or patiently transcribed material, back to the other side of the world, where the meticulous job of research could be extended, as an accompaniment to a university teaching career with some of the best colleagues I have ever known.

But at first it was a lonely time. I took myself on various trips to the far northern parts of the Northland, and remember visiting a cavernous wooden and corrugated-iron roofed shed in the middle of the bush, a place called Waggoner's Museum, in which the detritus of generations of New Zealand families had been accumulated, some from the 19th century, other things from recent decades: wagons, carts, old framed pictures, washing machines, spin dryers, items of furniture, gramophones. The guide took our group over to a working turntable and placed upon it a black shellac 78 rpm record, lifted over the heavy arm and lowered the needle onto it. Through the scratches and rustle the thin voice of Harry Lauder spun up into the air: 'Keep right on to the end of the road, keep right on to the end...'

I was invited to travel with 100 students from the Department of Maori Studies at the university on a visit to several Marae – meeting halls – in the Taranaki area, then over to the East Cape. This was an immersion into a different culture entirely, deeply salutary in terms of its self-respect and self-determination. From the rising Maori linguistic and cultural self-confidence, there was much to be learned. Courtesy and challenge were intertwined in the invitation. The Head of the Department interviewed me keenly, asking what sort of cultural tourist did I think I was? When I had made my assurances, he handed me some documents I was to read about Maori civilities on the Marae. Then he leaned forward intently: 'There *is* protocol,' he said emphatically. 'And you *will* make mistakes.' He paused. 'And you will be forgiven.'

There was also the travelling between one home and another, wanderings in other parts of the world, where I would be a guest, a visitor, a stravaiger. Adventures in America, Australia, Singapore, Samoa. Other stories. Nothing was assured. The master plan was not known to me. Which provided a kind of tension, a suspense. I remember those years of the 1980s and 1990s as culturally very distinct from our contemporary 21st century. Mass-media Anglo-American celebrity culture is instantaneous, the sparkler firework that distracts the eye as it fizzes evanescent lines in the black air. But immediate gratification abjures tension. Dynamics exist in language that are killed by slick reward. What stories I encountered included those of Maori cultural regeneration and New Zealand's national self-determination as a bilingual, multicultural, nuclear-free country. These were the results of long effort and consolidated public disposition.

In 1986, when I arrived, the Prime Minister David Lange was

saying No in thunder to nuclear weaponry and nuclear power, in defiance of the pressures from America and Australia to conform. The Greenpeace ship, the *Rainbow Warrior* had been blown up by French agents with murderous loss of life, and had been raised to be towed out and sunk as an underwater memorial and ocean-bed sea-haven. On my first visit to Auckland, walking down by the harbour, there she was, moored up and leaning. Whatever the distances, New Zealand seemed central to what mattered in the world.

After the first two months of the first year, I asked my mother to find the box with my poems and post it to me. Auckland University Press in New Zealand and Oxford in England published the first book, *This Folding Map*. A second book of poems arising directly from the very singular experiences of that first year in New Zealand followed, *An Open Return*. The third book, *First & Last Songs*, collected love poems and elegies, new co-ordinate points as they were discovered in New Zealand, and a deepening response to the loss of loved ones in Scotland. Ending the New Zealand chapter, the fourth book, *Clearances*, also published both there and here, appeared after we had come back to live in Scotland.

There is the time of departure and there is the return. David Balfour turns the key in the door and sets forth. The prodigal, after a long time walking up and down in the world, makes the safe harbour, or put it like this: Jason and the Argonauts make their way back with the treasure of the Golden Fleece intact.

For a while.

The two images work their magic at either end of the spectrum of the voyaging. The first one tells us: there is no Homecoming. There is no way back. But the second one says something else: the earth never really lets us leave. Wherever you go climbing or walking, in the mountains of Scotland or China, below the distant Sierra Nevada in Mexico or along the gentle ridge of the Malvern Hills in England, the earth breathes up from its terrain, and your reach for an infinite sky is never far enough. When Prokofiev ended his exile in the USA and left to return to Stalin's Union of Soviet Socialist Republics, accepting the risks and counting the cost, he knew what his own Russia meant to him. You can hear not only the sentiments of hope and longing but also the preciseness and exactitude of decision in the beautiful *cantilena*, the central, *andante assai* movement of his second violin concerto of 1935. When you listen to it, you can understand how irrevocable, haunting and piercing such music and meaning can be. This is the work of a man committed to returning home, even at the risk of his life, and willing to embrace such risk. The music is cheerful, for it resides in the knowledge of that home, not only Russia, but art itself. The great conductor Bruno Walter once commented, 'Napoleon is dead. Beethoven lives.' To paraphrase: 'Stalin is dead. Prokofiev lives.'

For home is also what you come to, what you arrive at, what you make, finally, a place called the Rest-and-be-Thankful. David has his inheritance. Still with a prospect, from which you depart on other journeys, but yet with a value for others, a place friends might visit, an open door to those you would welcome, a door firmly closed to those you will resist. Let's give it a name and a national provenance – Stevenson again: writing to the novelist S. R. Crockett, from Saranac Lake in the Adirondacks, New York State, USA, Spring 1888:

> Don't put 'N. B.' in your paper: put *Scotland*, and be done with it. Alas that I should be thus stabbed in the home of my friends! The name of my native land is not *North Britain*, whatever may be the name of yours.

And if that home were large enough to contain multitudes, then to return to it would be to want to make it better, to see it in the 'starry separateness' of independence. No diamond shines in all its multi-faceted beauty, until it's free from the earth. The quisling timidities shackling that vision, you try to identify, and to resist. A spine is what you stand up with. An openness of mind, and play, the quizzical, questions, all keep the dialogue fresh. Home is what connects you. All adults are in exile from their childhood. But every one of us will carry our childhood with us, for better or worse. Grown men are just wee boys. But if you can, you learn a little.

When I was a boy in Calderbank in Lanarkshire, there was a baker's shop in Airdrie, where I was born, named with a name you couldn't pronounce by seeing it, unless a local person told you. Fresh bread rolls for breakfast, or sometimes bought last thing at night, the odour of hot baking and flour filling the air, for clandestine suppers with mischievous uncles and grandparents up till all hours, were wrapped up in a white paper bag, on which was a blue line-drawing of a grinning horse, lying on its back, wriggling its legs in the air, under the slogan, 'There's nothing like a good roll!' Like Waggoner's Museum in New Zealand, Dalziel's is now gone, a family business lost in time. No such paper bags exist any more, but in my mortal memory, and now here. Other names hold secret visions and voices too: placenames like Milngavie, of course, and Strathaven, but better yet, because less known, Drumelzier and the Powsail burn. You'll find them in the pages that follow. What can be heard in music that cannot be seen is also part of the story, what makes whatever home might be. Voices you will welcome, those you will resist.

'Why do you want to go back to live in Scotland?' a friend asked me a month or two before we left.

I thought seriously about this for a moment but answered quite quickly, 'Because of the way people speak there.'

He saw I was serious and shook his head. 'You'll have to do better than that.'

It was true but there is always more to it, of course. A story my Uncle John once told me might help. A friend of his had been driving in the Highlands, and coming down a hillside, saw a full-grown deer standing in the field next the road. He parked the car quickly and quietly got out, took his 0.22 rifle and shot the beast at once, dragging it over to the road and placing it in front of the car, which he then drove over the deer, before lifting it manfully into the boot. A mile or so down the road, a police car drove up behind him, lights began to flash and he was pulled over. The knock at the window. He rolls it down. 'Excuse me sir, but do you realise there are four feet of a deer sticking out of the boot of your car?'

'Indeed I do, officer,' he says. 'You'll know the road back there comes down the hill and takes a steep curve quite suddenly at the bottom. When I came around that turn I was driving quite slowly but the deer was standing there, right in the middle of the road, and I'm afraid I knocked it down and drove over it, and I couldn't leave it lying there so I thought I'd better take it with me, so I lifted it into the boot of the car.'

'Do you mind if I have a look in the boot of your car, sir?'

'Not at all, officer.'

And they open up the boot.

After a swift examination, the policeman says, 'Do you realise sir that there is a 0.22 rifle lying there next to this deer?'

'Indeed I do.'

'And there is a 0.22 bullet-hole between its eyes?'

'Indeed yes, officer, I do. You see, when I ran over it I didn't kill it outright and luckily I had my rifle with me so I immediately put the poor creature out of its misery.'

'Aye,' says the policeman. 'On you go then, sir.'

And on he went.

Another story told to me by a friend in the small scattered community of Abriachan, on the shores of Loch Ness, just south of Inverness, on 30 April 2009, might help further. In the Second World War, many young men from the Highlands and Islands of Scotland joined the army and became snipers. They were excellent shots because of the practice they'd had with the deer. On one occasion a sniper was out in No-Man's Land and spotted a tree he could climb and keep a good lookout from, and he did that. After a while, sitting snug on a branch with his back to the trunk, staring out into the pitch-black night, he began to hear breathing nearby and he slowly realised there was another man hiding in the same tree beside him. At some point, the man whispered to him and he replied. Both spoke in Gaelic and each recognised by the other's voice the area he had come from. They never saw each other and did not exchange their names before they parted. Years later, at home, the man's father had died and he was the oldest man in the house, and another man came to see him to courteously ask permission to ask his sister to marry him. They recognised each other by voice alone. It took them some time to work out that they'd never seen each other, or knew each other's name, but their memories were precise enough to track their voices down to the encounter in the tree on that obsidian night in wartime.

Why should these stories make me feel at home? Let me try to answer by reference to what I take to be an axiomatic truth. The poet and translator Peter McCarey puts it like this in his essay, 'Language, Politics, Policy':

> Knowing who you are and where you are from is not only a matter of being able to say things to your friends without being understood by foreigners, useful though that can be at times.
>
> There are two main functions to speech: communication and identification. One function conveys messages and the other shows where the messages come from. One makes bridges and the other draws borders, often between two people who are trying to talk to each other. Both are vital.

Like any other book of good poems, hopefully, in *Homecoming* you can drop in anywhere, find something that has its own integrity and gives you liking, something you can carry. But *Homecoming* has its own carefully arranged trajectory as well, and the book can be read according to an arc of movement I have deliberately set out to emphasise. 'You should never explain a poem,' said William Carlos Williams, 'but it always helps.' Likewise a book.

The poems in this book were written over a period of almost a decade, begun before I left New Zealand – in fact, the first poems of the seven 'Preludes' were begun in the first years of my residence there, in 1988 – and ending with poems completed in 2009. So chronologically there is an overlap with the previous books and the beginning of this one. But *Homecoming* really gets underway with the affirmations of 'The Prospect' and the poems collected in the sections entitled 'The China Memorandum' and 'Other Places' which were prompted by the excursions of wandering around the planet I was fortunate enough to engage on in the first decade of the present millennium. The final section of the book returns to the home-nation. A little explanation of the overall context will be helpful here.

In the epigraph to this introduction, the irresistible good humour of the Nigerian Nobel laureate chimes with the feeling of confirmation whenever I return to Scotland. I would welcome the day when the airline pilot informs us that we are entering the Scottish airspace, and look through the porthole for Edwin Morgan's ships cruising along the border on the Solway Canal, under bridges, past friendly passport control points. But this is not simply a matter of warm pride and blessed self-confirmation, delicate and vulnerable as those may be. Far less is it a matter of national superiorism of the racist variety to which some people remain susceptible, in Scotland as elsewhere. It is rather a sense that whatever location we favour or are born with, there is unfinished business here, matters that still need resolution, and in politics, cultural production, languages, civil society and habits of life, much remains to be fought for. No country ever bled more than Nigeria for its independence *after* that country's independence had been gained. Belonging requires more than sentiment. The natural concerns and responsibilities that come with place and connection, are what Soyinka's words remind us of. And they don't go away.

But from 1986 to 2001, the landscape had changed. Thatcher had gone, but not her curses. The Berlin Wall had come down, but the open performance of Beethoven's Ninth Symphony marking hope in the event was televised in New Zealand with mind-searingly crass advertisements crammed between each movement of the music, as if to remind you that there are evils in capitalism too.

With the more personal co-ordinate points, something in the character of poetry in Scotland had changed as well. It was my great good fortune to have known personally that generation of major poets: MacDiarmid, Sorley MacLean, Norman MacCaig, Robert Garioch, George Mackay Brown, Iain Crichton Smith and Edwin Morgan. In 2001, Morgan was the only survivor. Finding continuities from that generation into the futures we might make was Morgan's prerogative above all, and he remains an example to whom the dedication of this book offers a salute. He is the figure of forwarding.

Homecoming begins and ends on small islands at opposite

poles of the planet, and ranges widely through the world between them. It begins on Matakana island, off the coast of New Zealand, and ends on Skathach's lonely rock beside the Isle of Skye in Scotland. The seven 'Preludes' that open the book take their cue from a particularly intense experience of solitude, distance and time, and the strengths of connection that persist and develop through family, friendship and art.

The second section makes lyrical but absolute affirmations: the seasons, tenderness and loyalty in love and the struggle for self-determination. Included here is the 'Wallace Triptych', first commissioned for the Luath Press commemorative volume, *The Wallace Muse*, a striking but troubling claim for Scotland's independence. If there is anything in Scotland worth knowing about deeply, there is no distance to which it is unattached, runs the now almost proverbial phrase. If we need the border, we need it to be porous. So there is nothing narrowing about it. The diversity of language and terrain within it connects us outwardly to all the world, so the central sections of the book are wanderings, reports on experience, postcards home.

At the invitation of the artist and teacher Alexander Moffat, then Head of Painting at Glasgow School of Art, I travelled on an extended visit to China in November to December 2004, and the poems from that trip form 'The China Memorandum'. They were effectively commissioned, as the journey was a collaboration between arts institutions in Australia, China and Scotland, with the participation of an artist and poet from Australia, twenty artists and two poets from China, and ourselves. We were sent to the mountainous region around the Li River and asked to respond to our location in poems, paintings and drawings, which were to be presented in exhibitions in the Guangxi province and in the Central Academy of Fine Arts in Beijing. The drawings that accompany the poems are courtesy of Sandy Moffat, a small sampling from a larger portfolio. For myself, this was the first opportunity since arriving back in Scotland where I had two weeks to do nothing but look around and write, so the pressure to produce was fortunately matched by an upwelling of appetite for the work of writing. That work was intense. The night before the first exhibition we were all fully occupied, finishing the poems, translating them into Chinese (which involved explaining them, which in some cases led to rewriting), and having them painted as script onto large sheets of paper, to be framed and hung in a gallery occupying an entire floor of the building otherwise filled with the paintings and drawings by the artists, Chinese, Australian and Scots.

The fourth section of *Homecoming* is a series of poems reflecting on international locations: Mexico, Geneva, Istanbul, Finland, Berlin during World War ii, Wales, Ireland and England are all present in poems that present recognisable descriptions of places, yet also follow through an optimistic enquiry into the possibilities of growth in the potential of other nations. Music features strongly, with portraits and evocations of great composers, including Sibelius and Richard Strauss.

The final section of the book brings us back to Scotland, from Drumelzier, in the Borders, the burying-place of the old bard Merlin, to Orkney, and memories of Orkney bards, Edwin Muir, Eric Linklater and George Mackay Brown. There are other far places: the Isles of Harris and Lewis, and Tiree. This is a 'homecoming' that includes a number of unexpected visitors. The great American novelist Herman Melville makes a journey to Glasgow, the Russian poet Pushkin takes a nocturnal sleigh-ride through a Scottish winter landscape, the ghost of Shakespeare's Hamlet wanders the battlements of an Elsinore relocated to a Scots language idiom, Sherlock Holmes and Dr Watson embark on a surreal quest, and a child encounters snow for the first time in Ayrshire. That most English of great composers Edward Elgar takes a suite of poems to himself, a composite self-portrait of his various visits to Scotland, and the various parts of Scotland he visited. We can learn more about our own terrain by paying attention to the ways in which people from elsewhere have seen it.

Finally we reach another island, in the Atlantic, crossing a precipitous bridge from the Isle of Skye to a rocky outcrop where in a very distant past, the Celtic hero Cuchulain once learnt the arts of war from the woman Skathach.

The poems in this book ask, and begin to answer, the key questions about the idea of 'Homecoming': how do you create a home worth having? And where do you go once you get there? Cuchulain kills the son who returns to him. The father is the stronger, and the son withholds his name. The story is a fearful warning, but also prompts questions about what might have been. What if the son had given his name, or what if the father had been less imperious? What if the fatherland had crumbled into something else, a new dispensation? And if we were to find ourselves in this new possible country, how might the arts help us live? What are our co-ordinate points, the moments and places from which the poems arise?

They are found in the cross-hairs of our telescopic sights, the intersecting lines of moments and occasions that occur without manufacturing, that have no forward-plan, methodology or strategy, other than intuitive; and literal places and locations, in material reality, physically present in a bodily world, with all its pressures, exactnesses and buoyancy.

They are the cross-hairs of history and geography, a vertical sense of layered time, language and stories rising through generations and across cultures, and a horizontal sense of the terrain, the landscape or seascape or cityscape as a context for your own perspectives and encounters with others, some friendly, some not. The layered patterns emerge and the horizontal gives you balance, taking account of variations, movement. All language is a transport, all stories metaphorical, linear or polyphonic, depending where and when. Naming is confirmation, celebration, the laughter of children, identity confirmed, and love. We are responsible to the unborn. But people die, places disappear, even the names change. And you have to find ways to approach these realisations. As Sorley MacLean once told me, 'There are particular occasions where neither the pronunciation of a word nor the spelling of that word are of any significance at all.'

But the co-ordinate points help you with not only where you are but where you're from and where you're going, not only which way to go, but how to go, what equipment you'll need to take, when to travel light and quickly, and when to stop moving and build.

Closer than geography and time, actual places, other people, the most intimate contexts are words and silence – but there are different kinds of silence into which the words will enter: the echo chambers of islands and sea, the bowl and curve of valleys, mountain peaks and ranges, ocean depths, the high plains, geologies of earth, the polyphony of forests and cities, the virtues of company and solitude. The question is: What music might be made of them all?

So now let me offer the first invitation, to touch the paper gently, at the top left-hand corner, with finger and thumb, to turn the page without tearing it, patiently. Let the words work, in their own time and tension and frame.

Open the door. Keep climbing. Find out.

I
SEVEN PRELUDES

On the Island

Matakana, 1988

It wasn't the words. There wasn't
any meaning to them. In the bar,
I thought, Have it your way. But then,

You were there in that
dark night, starless,
after the blaze of inside,
the long road home was not
to be seen in that blackness.

Your voice was a nearness, a guide
I had to keep close to, to keep
to the road. The fields on either side —
And gradually,
        the light began to allow me
to see your shape, against the island's rim,
the ocean beyond —

        And here, long after your death,
that there was that gradual way —
to find a way of seeing in that dark,
as if there was no reason even now
to be afraid of it.

October 1st, 1988

Oh father, father gone among —

There is no harbour
and no sunlight
the span of the bridge is not there

Absence is a fixed date
in memory. Desire
is what we'll have to plan for now

There are no big ships
and no-one there to pilot them
we have disembarked —

Then
Suddenly you are speaking to me
and your voice
is not as it was.

Dream Poem

I saw my mother's father once again the other night.
I haven't seen him often since he died.
He emerged from his shed (he was in it for hours
Through the night, enclosed in a nest of planks and beams,
  planes
And drills and saws and shelves and drawers of oddments,
Garden tools and implements). I'd sit on the roof as a boy, squat
Or hang from the edge like a monkey, run along the wall
By its side, beside the village church in Calderbank.
He was pushing his wheelbarrow, full of large stakes of firewood.
He was in shadow. Deeper shadows cast by the backyard lamp
Surrounded him. He held up a riddle from where it had lain
On top of the wood on the barrow. He held it up above his head
Like a chalice. He was offering it to us, me and my uncles and
  aunts,
Standing in the close-mouth. The wooden band was slightly split
And splintered. The wire mesh was still strong,
But caked and knotted and clotted with dried earth. Suddenly
He reminds me of King Lear, looking at his three daughters,
Leaning over the outrolled map of Britain, holding out
A single crown, and waiting for an answer.

Where?

At three, James points to the map and I ask him,
'Where do Nana and Grandpa live?'
'In Scotland,' he says, and points to it. 'They are Scottish.'
'And where do Grandma and Grandpop live?'
'New Zealand,' he says, and looks across the world,
and points to it. 'In Whangarei.'
'And where do we live?'
'In New Zealand.'
'But we are Scottish too,' he says,
and looks up expectantly with wide blue eyes,
the voice raised up at the end of the phrase, New Zealand
intonation, a question mark unspecified,
too far away to be hopeful
of any firm reply.
'Yes,' I tell him. 'We are Scottish.'
He's been there twice, started moving, crawled, fast,
from standstill to speed that first visit,
and then before we left,
a few steps, hesitant,
from his grandmother's hands to his mother's.
Now he sees the planes fly over
in different directions, all of them heading one way.
'Where is that plane going?' I ask him.
No hesitation, certainty impatient
with a question and answer so doubtless: 'To Scotland.'

By Doubtful Sound

The question was one
Of navigability: Whether
Or not there was a way
Out. Cook wondered at it,
Scanned the inlets, salt or fresh,
The Alpine slopes above,
Narrowing from present place
To distances, to terminal points.
He decided against it, but
Named the place before he left,
And the name held fast.
By Doubtful Sound
Our bearings balance counter-
Wise, South Island folds
Like cards against the North.
Let's shuffle the deck.
My love and I will look
Upon each other on the beach
At Doubtless Bay, these
Summer months, December
Through to March: only
Glad at moments we can
Spare, to take what necessity
Gives, to remember
Roads not taken,
By Doubtful Sounds.

The Gate of the Year

Midnight strikes, as usual.
The nursing home lights are dimmed by 10.30,
                    as usual.
Morgan goes to the window
and opens the curtains,
and the fireworks go off in the sky as the bells ring out,
                    as usual.
And none of these things will happen again,
like that.
            None of these things
                will happen again.

Mahler 10: Adagio

Transcription for Piano by Ronald Stevenson

It starts where everything begins to say goodbye, like that last night
before you had to leave. You go to your grandparents' bedroom,
to say goodnight, to try not to leave,
to stay awake, stay up, to make time last.
Last things always all too quickly over far too fast.

It starts with a touch, one finger then another,
one key then another, a cadence, a chord,
the sound holds on, subsides and rises, growing
more intense, rising to extremity
and then the hardest loneliness of all —

after all that is older and lonely, attached to it all by
precision and love. To occupy the air
like time, like silence, after you've gone, hold on
with this, like this, like this. Like this.

2

THE PROSPECT

'Why not *really* blow it up, Captain?'

Manifesto

The sun nails his credentials on
the wooden door of day
a morning manifesto: wake up!
the First of May —

Revolution — well,
this was the first.
What followed failed
but this persists.

All This

for Rae

Something is lifting —

your shape in the air

      light   rising

your hair

your skin as you smile

there

      all this while

Wallace Triptych

1   After the Battle

Wallace knelt down, before the bleeding man.
The salt grass brushed his calves.

The dying man looked up at him, eyes
keen. Proximity
      was everything.

Wallace let his left hand steady himself, fingers
outstretched, fingertips
      on the earth between the grassblades.

The English eyes turned round to him, afraid.
Wallace had seen them already, started to
wipe his fingers on the grass, forgiving
and condemning in that touch.

What I care about now,
      is not to do with this
(ice in the heart of winter, mind elemental snow)
No. Nor can it be more abstract.
      (Language, life, a world more full
      of what there is than all that
      I could learn)
No. What I care about now,
he said, is what I can do,
what I can do for this good.

The border is there, and needed.

He rose and turned,
into a seam of sunlight on the hills.
'Skin him,' he said.

There is, this —
a cruelty, required?

Decisively.

2   *Abstract*

It is the fact they had to make him *Sir* —
He was common. He was
of the people.

And then the passion in those learned hands
grasped on the handle,
swinging that sword.

That *there* might be the room for us to be
in all the creativity
we need.

And all the men and women in the country
might have the words and air
to breathe their lives in.

He stands like Burns, will always stand, *for*
correction of the folly and the false,
to kill the aristocracy

and end the farce of that distinction
always. The lifting of the head.
The honesty.

3   *At Stirling Brig*

This shilpit nation, set against itself
I'll make complete, and fit to speak to others
independently.
       Rax me the hilt o' that sword!
Whit sang is this?

His hearing took the sounds
of languages and music in cathedrals, voices raised
to magnify by stone. He nodded and approved,
his muscles tensing, knowledge of the prospect bringing
fear and resolution. *People of Scotland, now.*

       And nimbleness, the unpredicted element.
The form of church and righteousness.
The variedness of folk, and words.

These things are brought to this:
Wallace on horse, the spearsmen
ready, blood crusted on the blades —

The bridge. The water running. Brightness.
The prospect.

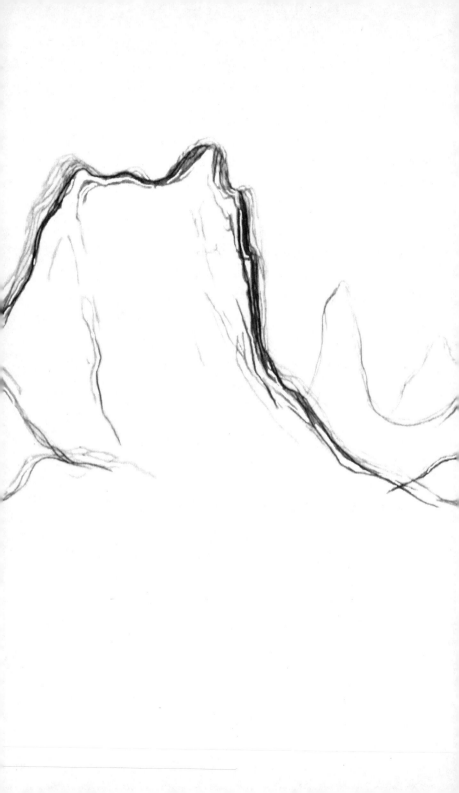

3

THE CHINA MEMORANDUM

The Protestant View

That eternal dissent
and the ravages of
faction are preferable
to the voluntary
servitude of blind
obedience.

EDWARD DORN

The Memory

Lonely wakeful nights of childhood: one —
unrestful on an historical mattress,
with a smile on my face of delight and astonishment,
under the weight of a green silk quilt,
my grandfather asleep on the right,
the room in shadow, visible, as a car at the corner turning outside
casts headlight-beams in a big yellow arc over the ceiling:
the brown-gold, wedged-glass chandelier,
the furniture against the walls surrounding us,
lit up for a moment, as the shadows swing around.

My grandfather, when he'd come in,
after I'd gone to bed, had grinned at me, leapt
onto the bed, bounced to the bedside cabinet,
leapt to the top of the wardrobe,
stepped off and onto the mantlepiece twice lightly
then over the tallboy, onto the bedside table,
finger-tipped the chandelier so it swayed like a Hollywood bowl
as he threw himself bodily over me
to his side of the bed and called
'Good night!' and gone to sleep.
His black silk Chinese smoking-jacket
hanging very neatly, on this side of the door.

The Exchange

Taking tea at midnight
beneath the mild November moon
in tentative company
on the veranda
overlooking the river, with three peaks
behind, and an arc of them
before, in the serried and segregating light
of that moving moon.

A single white spot,
far away through tree-trunks and reeds,
is a night-fisherman out on the river
invisible in the dark.

The Technologies

The woman with the cormorants
sits beside the stone pier
as the 4-pole bamboo raft pulls up —

We disembark as the young man
disappears with his shiny silver camera and
there are tables and trays
of crispy hot shrimps and tiny crabs
on wooden skewers by the riverside.

And in the tent behind the truck by the roadside
the computers are printing by the time you've
crunched your shrimps,
with the laminated photo snapped
when you stepped off the raft two minutes ago.

Technologies cross centuries:
the currency of now.

The Encounter

To have taken the boat downstream
to the village, and to find
the narrow path up through the bamboo barricade
beyond the stony beach
where a young woman is hacking at the washing
on a stone by the waterside —
to have found the pathway's entrance
to the village blocked by villagers
who close in sharply and block our way,
letting three of us go on, cutting two of us off,
demanding more money, approaching to inches
away, and suddenly the woman standing nearest,
knitting woollen sandals for the tourists
turns into something else, and the men
are a couple of feet away, and another
group are waiting up the path, and the closer
ones are quickly
shaking open hands to warn us
away, get lost, get going, go
unless you pay more money, and
if we do, what of the other group?
The shouting starts to rise,
the women yelling angrily,
the men very agitated, the gestures
violent. The nearest woman's knitting needles
seem awfully close, and ready to get closer
were it not for the value she sets upon

the object she is knitting. The three ahead come down.
'Too much hostility,' Robert breathes. He's right.
'No point in trying to go through there. Not
like that.' We back away,
walk down to the beach once again,
sit on a bamboo raft, drawn up on the pebbles by the shore.
The young woman down at the watermargin
carries on hacking her washing.

On the Telephone

Standing in Xing Ping,
in the street, the filthy, dusty drag of it
the high mountains all around it, in the heat,
on the telephone,
talking to my wife, in the green, wet, leafy cold
of late November Scotland.
She's getting the boys ready for school
at half-past-eight in the morning.
I speak to my children each in turn
James, 10, and David, 6, asking them
what present they would like
me to bring them from China?
Each of them in turn
enunciating every syllable
carefully, tells me: 'Anything,
Daddy, except a book.'

— I shall go to the Ghost Market
in Beijing, and buy
two small iron dragons for them,
that they might guard their wisdom
and protect their independence.

The Likeness

Once upon a time,
my grandmother
poured salt into a cellar,
held it upside down,
not noticing the top was open
and of course the salt poured through,
making a perfectly conical mound on the table.

I was a wee boy, looking over the table's rim
and that hill of salt
was exactly
the shape
of that mountain.

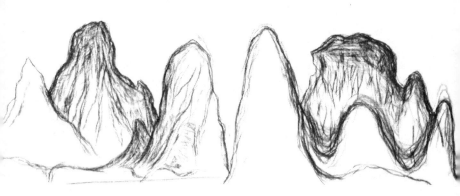

A Catalogue of Mountains

Sometimes mountains look the other way,
steaming off into the further distance,
occasionally turning to admonish you,
to keep up. Suilven is like this. Some
mountains seem to be completely in the present
tense, evoking the world, in time and space,
massively various, yet knowable by appetite
and energy, increasingly by skill, by knowledge in
the places of them, by a tender balancing
of familiarity and respect. Blaven is like this.
(Ben Dorain too, it soars and sings,
though all its forests have gone now.)
Some move in different trajectories, netting them
across themselves, at different heights, so that
you rise steeply, then cross a saddle
laterally, then climb along a lifting ridge,
move through forest, up around and over the scree,
along a lifting arc, reach the sharp peak, the
summit, accomplish the entire traverse. The hill of winds,
Arran's lean Goatfell, I remember that way. Others circle
and recircle and the circles overlap. Think of
Salisbury Crags and Arthur's Seat, or the
intrinsically mysterious shape of the Eildon Hills,
the wizardry by which they were formed.

But here in China, these hills all reach upwards urgently,
aspire, lift, scale, sheer, tip and peak,
foliage and trees are their adornments,
beads and bangles, necklaces and fringements.
The rock itself is always moving upwards.

The Magnetics of Earth

The pinnacles rise all around us, into the light.
The trucks sound like motor-boats,
small cargo boats, plying up and down
the river of the street.
The voices of the men are dockers' cries,
market cries, like harsh, competitive bells.

The bamboo groves behind the schoolhouse roofs
and the teachers' flats
spear straight up. Beyond them, the pinnacles
strike upwards for clear air,
looking for more sky
through blue-gold haze —
A sisterhood of rising shapeliness.
A brotherhood of strange familiarities,
slanted by distortions in their growth,
twisted, as families are, by
love and difference, cruelty and friendliness and force.

I climbed this morning by a simple staircase
cut in the rock
to where the stone was vertical, iron ladders bolted
to concrete walls, handholds, footholds, taking you further
upwards, the effort of rising
      in the upper torso
      as the effort would be
      in the lower torso, ankles and legs,
      in the descent.

Reaching the pagoda at the top, the summits all around,
I wanted to keep rising,
to keep going on
while the karst was easy to grip, fixed and
settled, and secure.

Suddenly it was as if
what binds us breathed up from below,
through bushes and trees,
to whisper that the earth
will never really let us leave.

The summit is pointed and curved
by its magnet.
The sky is not enough.

Four Poems from the Village of the Autonomous People

I

all the way
through
the original dark
of the night

I've been listening to
the water on   the bamboo
surrendering   waterwheel
uplifting itself   turning
as it goes through   as slowly
as the river
running below, as it goes through, uplifting itself, surrendering
its watering

2

In the day –

                I waken on a board
                hard as the wood I'll lie on
                after all

The sawmill behind me on the hillside
throws out its snarls
and streaming growls, familiarly

Slowly, one
by one
the villagers walk from the village,

carrying a plank or two,
a saw, some tools
      to walk to the pagoda
going along the edge of the road

3

By the Bridge of Wind and Rain

        on the long road as it curves around

the contours of the hills —

It is the unobtrusive pace
        the motion of it all —

the waterbuffalo moves in its own time

        The pig squeals as it's dragged
        by the ears
        into the back of the truck

River, valley, people —

        It rests on this
        Rising from where I was
        to rest on this.

4

No. It rests on this:

The men on the roadside standing with the fuse
in their hands, the rubble all around,
the plans unfolded open
on a big white rock beside them,
a long drive away
from the place of Autonomous people —

      to dynamite the mountain, open it for roads
      traffic, speed, connections, for factories,
      spilling into the pastoral
      like a heap of sawdust falls or oil or blood stains hands

extinguishing the etiquette of movement
in places that need everything but this —

The Mother speaks to her Son

When you come home from the city to your village
you tell me nothing about where you live now.
Your clothes must be different there. You are wearing
the old style here. But things seem changed somehow.

The buffalo walk by the river as usual
and the mist suffuses the valley as the tea crops
surround the slopes on the terraces. This is normal.
Your eyes return to the road outside the gate, and to the
   mountain-tops.

You walk among your people once again at the turn of the year
and you will not speak to me of your life away from here.
The light in your eyes this morning smooths yesterday's lines
   from your brow.
And my love is undiminished, though you are a stranger to me
   now.

The Surprise

Deep in the middle of my seventh night in China,
in the village of the Autonomous People of Dong,
away in the northernmost hills of the Province of Guangxi,
the costumes and performances flamboyant, the final dance
farewell, the music made vigour seem bright,
all fun and fast fraternity, soaring up,
beneath the deepest blue, the housefronts echoing
shrilly, wind and wood, no wonder when the leader took us
into that formation looping underarms and threading through
the circled group in what seemed then abandonment,
the singing and the dancing rose and circled in to pull me
to its centre, suddenly, from standing still to lifted, prone,
my horizontal body thus propelled, upwards,
entirely disconnected from the earth
in deep mid-air, in thickest midnight blue,
under an approaching rush
of stars, before gravity brought me back to welcoming hands
three times, each one higher,
and the grinning faces of the circled crowd below me
matched the stars in brightness
when they put me on my feet again
in the middle of that concrete village square,
firmly, standing, trembly, under every gentle glitter,
in a waving ring of laughter, on that fine night.

The Wall

At Mutianyu

The Great Wall —
                the silence of it
and a warm sun
                on the cold trees
the crisp leaves holding on and fluttering
in the blue air
                that deep brown bushy squirrel, almost black,
moving fast
                across the steep-diving path,
and into the wild, crossing
                from one side
to the other —
                the silence of it all
                the lunar cold
in the unquenchable thirst of want,
that anger, driving men down —
like that moment from the still and sunshine on the path
ascending, when suddenly
the wind blew down from Mongolia,
you could hear and all but see it
come from the desert
over the far summits, down the broken
slopes, running or riding like a horde of unknowable
horsemen, cold as inhuman things are,
coming at you, up to the wall
to pass or to be stopped —

'Only when I am here,' said our guide
'do I feel the greatness of my ancestors.'

making us think of those
           who built it, brick by brick, stone by stone
           then built it and rebuilt it once again
           and died beneath it, bones in the earth
           hard below the skeletal trees
           by the broken rocks and ridges of the summits.

The Forbidden City

the shock
opulence provides
the minimalist repetition
of harmony prevails
and so on

while high above the spot on the floor
where the general stood to report
the steel ball was waiting
locked to the ceiling,
waiting for the moment
when the emperor decided
if the news was not to his liking
to trip the switch,
drop the ball
crush the bad
news with the newsman's
head. Harmony prevails. Mop up the stains.

Get that eunuch
to hold the old wife
head down in that harmonizing well
and put the lid on her feet. So much
for embarrassment.
And when the other army's at the gate,
you top yourself,
don't hang around.

I asked our guide: 'When I
first came here, eight years ago,' he said,
'I was shocked. The wealth was all for itself.'
'So it was not the greatness of ancestors here
that impressed you?' I asked.
'Not greatness. No. The selfish wealth of it
and cruelty,' he said.
Now we walk beneath
the portrait of Mao, and through
gate after gate,
room after room,
broad courtyard after courtyard,
where such things were done.

The Ghost Market

Teapots giant frogs dragons lions ashtrays steaming
rice and noodles glimpsed in chopsticks on the way from
bowl to mouth great croichles in the throats and gobs
of phlegm and sneezes wiped with fingers to the pavement and
bracelets bangles necklaces and beads and statues carved
and jade and rugs and don't forget those human
skull-tops from Tibet and phallus, balls in black
cold stone and rows of dragons, camels, tigers, cigarettes
and smoke from men in corners each surrounded by their
boxes, stalls, and hanging screens and silks
and paper crinkled covered with calligraphy and little calls
of hard-sell chatter, crowds, the push, the clack, the clatter,
mah-jong, chopsticks, food, the Chairman Mao alarm-clocks and
the statuettes saluting and the bad old dusty books, the matter of
the market and it's all so real and fake and fast and furious,
running in the veins and the curious pause and push and pass
the avenues and corridors and lanes between the stalls
the women in their furry hats the men with pocket
calculators, held out in their open hands and
how much does it cost? how much will you pay?
how many objects here are on display?
how many people did you pass today?
how many ghosts walked through you on your way?

4

OTHER PLACES

You can work it out by Fractions or by simple Rule of Three,
But the way of Tweedle-dum is not the way of Tweedle-dee.
You can twist it, you can turn it, you can plait it till you drop,
But the way of Pilly-Winky's not the way of Winkie-Pop!

RUDYARD KIPLING, *The Jungle Book*

Mexico Poem: Tijuana Brass

Bienvenidos a Tijuana

(*Auntie Anna's Famous Brothel for* US *Marines from San Diego*)

Tijuana waxworks. Quiet in the lobby. The woman at the
   counter has no change
for a $20 bill. Back to the street. First, off Revolucion, the Sierra
   all around,
now pink and hazed bronze; you can pick up a trace of the
   silence from
the snow up there. The beat, though, is all along here: dance,
   silver, leather
whips? / you like whips? and hand-cuffs? sombreros all
   a-glitter in the evening sun,
the storefronts and the balconies all selling, and you've seen it all
   before, it's all
been done before, oh, so many times! how many times? The faces
   aged into
acceptance, weathered into humour and ways to get through,
the big mustachios, the shiny silver buckles, the cigars, the cars as
   big as helicopters,
the buses from before the Revolution, the filth and sell, the poor,
   and you walk
across the bridge across the Tijuana river, a thin band running
   straight

from the Sierra, one long silver line in its concrete channel, and
   all along the bridge
and the stairs up to it, and the stairs down from it, the children
   are there,
one every few yards, old women too, battering it out on crazy
   drums
in tune with something somewhere, like Gaelic singers singing
   psalms
in Lewis, an old man plays a lively tune on a harmonica with his
   one
right hand, he has no other one, or legs, his flinty flushing eyes
are speaking, looking up, the kids cry out with Abba's pace and
   emphasis,
'Man-ay, Man-ay, Man-ay – da daa – na na na na naah!'
El Mariachi songs, the brass of it all, like the waxworks I will
not get into now, having too much money to afford the entrance
   fee.
The Mexican flag hangs and runs out like water rippling in a
   huge diagonal,
an oblique oblong in the long slanting light of December,
   4.25pm, that
Pacific border light, no cloud, the dust and snow from the
   distance,
the feel of trafficking, now all around you, the sweet sugary smell
from the deepfried pastry, the meat frying for tortillas and the
   sour smell
of burning sweetcorn leaves by the vendors by the Cathedral in
   whose darkness
the grotto is a shrine to which a crowd of people raise their eyes
from scattered places in the pews, and a man on the corner of
   Revolooshyoan

is shouting into a microphone: 'No pasaran! No pasaran!'
And down in the empty concrete valley by the river, another man
   is walking
absolutely alone, under the footbridge, on towards the impossible
   mountains,
as if not one thing in the world could yet prevent him. Solitude in
   sandals,
grey suit, the jacket flapping open in the breeze. He does not
   look around.
Not even for a moment. What gives him such authority,
   direction? Hope?

At Chambésy

for Maria and Peter McCarey

From the veranda,
in the early evening light and with binoculars,
look over the trees on the shore, the railway
track, the calm expanse of Lake Léman and let your gaze
rise up above Geneva, towards the white.

The lenses tune the silence.

A passing train slides by.

In the ocular O of the spectacle
the distance shoots back through the retina, into the brain.

The high icefields, the sounds
that would be there, creaks, sharp cracks, the clash of pick
for handhold, foothold. The scale of it:
an arching amphitheatre of rugged ice,
a stroll across a snowfield could take a day, eternity,
a long time in a life of hours, to be on the edge.
The cliffs are sheer, perpetual. Here,
Frankenstein's monster shook his stolen limbs
and raged in silence.

Below these heights, the blue air blazing up,
inhumanly. That little group in Byron's house
cooked up their brains and out cracked sex
and violence. Every vein and sinew in its own
intensity.

While here at Chambésy,
the wooden floor and panelling are calming,
bookshelves steady as the hand that pours a gin
and tonic, the others waiting in the study,
sunny in the evening.

The Alpine ice; the fevered brains
And our sedate enquiries, sketching:
A delicate triangulation, balanced.

Let's leave it at that.

Five Poems from Istanbul

I   Love poem: missing you

As a new moon, she
steps down the marble staircase,
the mint pashmina bound
around her throat, tossed back,
a rising trail
buoyant, in the air
of laughter and light
conversation below —
her eyes are intelligence
her face, rose and pearl
        the scarf lifts its silk
as the moon would toss diamonds
over the grace of her orbit,
as slow as allurement, as sure
as the white
on the opulent water tonight.

And now in the gold-panelled hall,
the words on either side of her
are compliments, as if the frogs and insects spoke
applause along the riverbank,
like ripples on the basin rim
of a fountain, gold and
turquoise marble, round
the central dispensation —
her promise and possession in
this moving constellation.

It's only that you are not here
that makes the virtues and the facts
of all you are seem, wishfully, near.

2   *Chilling out in the breeze in Zekeriyakoy*

On the wooden chair on the wooden deck,
looking over the pool where the boys are splashing about,
into the sky all zipped around by house martins, up,
down and under the eaves, tearaway wee
arrowheads, dark blue speed in the azure, looking
over the rooftops towards the lifting horizon, my gaze
drifts back down from the heights, slowly
filters through the forested slopes, the trees,
the branches, small twigs, leaves,
the trails into the woods where
riding, we might go tomorrow,
and I'm letting the hillside forest
run like a comb through my mind
and the slow act of swimming begins:
I'll change and walk down the stone steps and path
to the pool where the boys are still yelling and jumping
and the noises too, will sift out things, and
there will be one simple dive
that takes us into a blue light
under the surface again, relaxed, not
East nor West but deep in the silent centre,
then up to the surface and splashing around.

3   *Istanbul Huzun / Melancholy Hit*

There is always a story,
another story, waiting to be told.
Driving by the waterside, the blue
choppy with currents and wind
and the sky big enough to encompass it all:
the big ships heading up the Bosphorus,
the Black Sea destination blue slate under grey.
And even in all this, the melancholy touch,
some item of news on the telephone, a hit,
a sadness that cannot be predicted or addressed,
some abstract feeling seeping through, beside
the maybe thirteen million
particular lives, in Istanbul.

Driving by the *yalli* by the waterside, they're all done up,
expensive, looking good, or else run down,
in tattered wood, the banisters and balconies
varieties of disrepair, all melancholic, full of
loss and attractiveness, as still
the boats and cars go up and down, and the market
does what it does. The long lines of roads by the waterside,
the long lines of shipping moving on the water,
the long and intricate patterns
of roads and tracks on hillsides steep as dreams
with impossible corners and heights, half-finished
concrete buildings, broken-down shanty-town shacks,
expensive estates of detached houses, all
so far spread out along the contours of
the distances allowed along the Bosphorus, and

Golden Horn: a city on the shape of its terrain,
populous in horizontals, shapely with its punctuating
domes and minarets. Even the sky pulls upwards and back
to hear those multitudinous voices call,
to be big enough to encompass it all.

4   *The trees that make the forest*

You need to go into the forest
at least once a year, to be lost
for a while, if you're lucky,
and find a way out,
at the last.
       In childhood, the forest seemed endless
walnut, oak wood, pine. Here in the garden,
the wind moves the leaves of the silver birch and that
Canadian maple, dark purple, almost black:
and the sound of each tree is different —
the maple, large swathes of *hush*, backed over
again, in layers of *hush*, *hush*, but the birch
has smaller leaves that tend to clatter
as they glitter on the long, spear-like branches,
like a lightweight rattle of scree, quietly,
on a mountainslope of air, away
in high places.
       In childhood, the forest was books
and words spilling into them, stories were hillsides
of sounds that washed over and into each other
like hopes and disappointments, and words

spilling out of them again, in time to show you paths,
methodologies of movement, ways
to get out, to begin to map the territory, gradients,
contours, in memory, in mind.
　　　　But here in the garden now,
you've come out of the forest again
and what you have to deal with are
the movements of linear time.

5　　*Connections*

The adults are the people on the tram,
running up the hill, into the city's maze
where they'll become pedestrians, and children once again.
What could they remember and retain of its complexities?
The city is a forest for us all, at times like this.
Take a line and follow it.
There are connections. Move.

At the Sibelius Monument, Helsinki

Let me hear that self-determination,
even in defeat, like the end of the first. And the end of the fifth:
Those vast triumphant chords, to which assent is all
that's not absurd. Let me never forget the silence
always ready to come down, in that 'gaunt, El Greco
emaciated fourth'. Or the sound of all creation,
continuous in seven, right to the edge.

And now I'm here: Those upright clustered pipes —
a massive, unobtrusive imposition,
silver metal tubes, like birch trunks, glittering steadily,
some of them bark-ragged, veins unzipped to the air,
opening earth to sky, bringing sky back to ground
uplifting the lightest sounds. —

The real trees move in the wind as it carries the sounds between
   them,
the children yelling in the schoolyard just nearby.
And your face as it stays a little distance away,
and nobody else is here
a shining apparition on this mild April day,
when the north is all a vast resource behind me, listening —
And a dog walks quietly over the gravel.

Helsinki

Crosswinds, cold currents, forests of crowds,
moving like tides coming in from the East
in the air, from the West and the South,
in the sea, and the spine of the North
attaches the mind to its root, touches the earth
as it opens the judgement of eye
and measuring wisdom, intelligent breath,
rocks, water, trees, naturally —

Nature compelled them too, and no élite escapes
encounter with the idle wind that tears the broken branch away,
the roof from the house, the old man from his family,
or time that withers too quickly
the young. The violent storm, north European winter.

The bully in the schoolyard can be beaten or constrained
but force is there in nature too, inimical to hope:
the accidental breaks across plans, creates
new structures. What made that urge to see as central,
in the whole nation's story, the life and work of Jean Sibelius?

Standing against force —
                          the Russian soldiers riding up the 47 steps
of stone before the Lutheran Cathedral, white
                          as snow, golden domed, the Cossacks on
their horses in the square, in 1905.
Here and now, young women and young men

walk on the southern coast of this far north, their hinterland
rising above them, a sweep of cloak, forest-green,
hard rock and icy water, a nation like a dark gown, warming,
on a day of strong weather.
Its strengths give its heavy material substance shape.
As mind and art through people make shapely their reality,
inhabiting their preferences:
flags, music, nation, resistances, form.

Penmachno

for Ruth and Tony Sullivan

This whitewashed cottage, roses startling pink on the outside
   wall,
is bathed in green Welsh valley light, this summer afternoon, as
   we go in.
'There's no back door,' says Tony, on the step, half-smiling, half
   in shadow.

The kitchen and the living-room have great blank whitewashed
   walls,
a cold slate fireplace, thin steep stairway leading to bedrooms.
Our youngest boy, now seven, races up to the window. 'There's
   David!' he shouts.

'That's me!' — The house backs up on the graveyard, looks across
the unmown hay grass waving by the leaning slates of headstones
and the church, over there, under the hill where the afternoon
   light is shadowy now

and the balance, front and back, seems fair. There's only one way
   out of here,
of course. *David Jones*, the headstone says, the rest in Welsh.
I teach our children *Thank you* in that language.

'Not you,' I tell the youngest. 'That's another David.' He's out
  already.
The front door leads back out. The playground they'll spend
  hours in,
swinging plastic swords, is a short walk to the left;

the swimming-hole by the bridge on the Machno river,
a longer walk the other way. They swim in it. We all do.
Bathe there in the sunlight, sleep beside the dead.

Bonanza

It is not brandy, it is not wine
It is Jameson's Irish Whiskey
It fills the heart with a joy divine
And it makes the fancy frisky.

JAMES ('B.V.') THOMSON

We passed Coleraine, got snarled up in traffic
at Toome Bridge, began to rise above the Glen Shane pass
to the highest pub in Ireland, so he said, *The Ponderosa*,
and present-moment mist got thick till all was dense in fog,
the dark come down and the headlights crossed, criss-crossed,
in the flow of the rise to the height
where a lonely sign by the roadside said, BAR. FOOD.
And a window showed a light like a ghost with a lantern.
We pulled the car over, drove into the empty
carpark, parked, got out, went in.

One old man on a stool drinking gin.
A woman behind the bar. We buy Guinness, two
pints please. ('Is this place...' I start to ask in a whisper)
A young man comes in from the back, in jeans
and orange T-shirt. 'There's your answer,' Patrick says.

Above the low, hot, smouldering fire,
domestic and fierce, a map is screwed to the wall:
Northern Ireland. The South curves up and around,
as you might see, looking out from a window, the South
as you're facing North. On the opposite wall,
at the furthest end of the room, another map —
Nevada, Lake Tahoe, a big triangular area shaded in:
The Ponderosa. There are signatures on it:
Lorne Greene. Dan Blocker. The actors from *Bonanza.*

The woman and the old man,
their voices drifting over:

'...See that man's *sperm count*...'

'...Well,' (the old man's intimate, loud whisper)
'...I can tell ye, *my* sperm count is *high*...'

— In the toilet, above the urinal, there's a poster that reads:
'Don't just stand there. Start a business of your own. Now.'
Contact details provided. From every window, the night
is black. The fog, impenetrable. Over four windows,
the curtains are drawn.

Beside the map of Nevada,
framed, are mounted six six-inch lines
of different kinds of barbed wire. Each is named.
Each is twisted differently, barbed differently.
Each is black with rust and the paper they are mounted on
is brown with soaked-through nicotine, it seems.

These are the names:

>H.H. Frye, 'Parallel Lines'
>
>A.S. Burnell, 'Hooked Barb'
>
>J. Haish, 'Original S Barb'
>
>E.M. Crandal, 'Zig-Zag'
>
>C.E. Sunderland, 'Kink'
>
>J.F. Glidden, 'Winner'

The legend at the top says,
'The wires that fenced the west.'

The Speechless

remembering: 60 years since Hiroshima and Nagasaki

The courting doves in the tall trees alight, grey
on the high branches. The light on the green leaves
dapples them yellow, shadows the grey down
on doves' backs, wing-feathers folded.

The blue tits come to the sapling in the corner
of the garden, jab at the nuts in their net cylinder,
flit back and forth, neurotic by habit and need.
The coal tit comes, and in its season too, the robin.

One day the garden fell silent. The cushioning song
of the grey doves, calling each other; the small songs of others,
the caw of the crows and the far calls of seagulls, ended.
The buzzard sat on the fencepost, looking around.

A sense of unreturning absences surrounded it,
unrecoverable knowledge: patterns, songs and sounds.
Like rain from the black cloud, filling the air,
bringing no good, drowning the knowable,

ending the sounds in its downpour,
ending the different languages, all our conversations,
ending life's distractions and its detail.

The Confrontation

'The essence of propaganda consists in winning people over to an idea so sincerely, so vitally, that in the end they succumb to it utterly and can never again escape from it.'

GOEBBELS

'The film is to America what the flag once was to Britain. By its means Uncle Sam may hope some day, if he be not checked in time, to Americanize the world.'

The London Morning Post (1923)

'He said that the great offensives of the future would be psychological, and he thought the Governments should get busy about it and prepare their defence... He considered that the most deadly weapon in the world was the power of mass-persuasion.'

JOHN BUCHAN, *The Three Hostages* (1924)

Richard Strauss went to Berlin in 1941,
to discuss the matter of royalties and the rights of composers
of classical music, as opposed to popular music.
As president of the Reichsmusikkammer,
Strauss had declared in 1934 that composers of 'serious' music
   (*ernste Musik*)
should get a higher percentage. Goebbels overruled that directive.
Strauss responded that the Propaganda Minister had no right
   to interfere
in the affairs of composers. He went to see Goebbels about it.

He was taken up directly to Nazi high command,
where he received a tongue-lashing loud enough to be heard
well beyond the closed doors. Goebbels ordered that a letter
that had been written by Strauss should be read aloud:
'As for the authorized statute concerning royalties,
we ourselves shall decide the question of distribution,'
Strauss had written.
'Goebbels has no right to interfere.'
Goebbels slapped at the letter and screamed:
'Herr Strauss did you write that?'
'Yes.'
'Silence! You have no idea who you are and who I am!
You dare to call Lehár a street musician?
I can feed this impertinence to the press...
Lehár has the masses and you don't!
The art of tomorrow is different from the art of yesterday.
You, Herr Strauss, are from yesterday!'
Strauss left the meeting shaken and on the edge of tears.
He now knew that fame and humiliation were sharply placed
    together,
that he had no way to protect his own family
and that even shut off in his mansion at Garmisch,
reading Goethe, writing memoirs and essays and music,
the realities of politics would keep invading his world.
In 1941 he was seventy-seven years old.
Goebbels was forty-four.

At the end of the war, American soldiers arrived in Garmisch
by 30 April, the day of Hitler's suicide. The larger villas were
    being taken over

and used for the quartering of troops. The old composer went
    out to his front gate
and said, 'I am Richard Strauss, the composer of *Der
    Rosenkavalier* and *Salome*.
Please leave me alone.' But as luck would have it, sitting in
    the jeep
was an American officer who knew Strauss's music.
They declared the villa off-limits and safe.
And one of the American soldiers who visited him there
was a 24-year-old musician named John de Lancie,
principal oboeist with the Pittsburgh Symphony Orchestra,
and the shy, young de Lancie asked whether Strauss had
    ever thought
of writing a concerto for his instrument.
'No,' was all Strauss said.
But the oboe concerto was then begun
and first performed in February, 1946.

It has none of the horrors of war.
It breathes the clear air of Mozart.
It speaks of the things of the past
that but for the work of the artist
the future might have destroyed.
It speaks of the act of giving.
It is Strauss's great gift to us,
and the soldier who asked the right question.

The Impossible

It must have been about a year
later, after I put down the phone
that night.

      It wasn't the anger
or the agony of the thing.
I could have carried that as you did.
It was the pity in your voice
that bit my pride. I could not hold on that
for you, for any longer.

      But it was about a year
later, in another country
in a different continent
and I saw you driving a car,
coming out of a side-road, a lane
surrounded by bushes, pausing
and peering to left and to right
and right again, as I was approaching
and passing, driving towards the roundabout
and on, knowing that it wasn't you,
it couldn't have been you, and yet still, now,
I go back to that moment, to remember
you, that parting, the words,
the bitterness and love,
the impossible, unanswered.

The Warren

The steep approach, from the high grass slopes,
Allows you a map, if you keep your eyes on the other side,
On the far park, where the bushes are,
As you're walking down to the road.

But once across and rising on the other side of the valley,
Your step on the short dry grass, your eyes on the approaching
Bushes, the view is not what it was from the heights:
It's a warren. A path leads you in.

The bushes become clustered, the paths branch out,
The bushes surround you, higher than your eyes,
Thicken around you. The paths become intricate,
Winding back, reconnecting. Now

You can no longer see back, over to the other side, over
The tops of the lower bushes. They're all too high.
All you have to go on now is the rising slope
Of the hillside. You keep climbing.

Diagonally moving upwards, the only co-ordinates left beside
The contours under your feet, are the sun and the breeze
And what you might remember
Of the lie of the land you saw, from the other side.

If you become entangled and bewildered, you retrace your steps.
The paths circle round. The bushes are close to each other.
Sometimes you have to come up another way. Keep climbing.
Press through. Keep climbing. Find your way out.

The Two Travellers

for Adrian Mitchell, 1932–2008

It was on an island on the other side of the world
A long, long time ago and I remember our two friends
They were talking to each other, about him —
In a friendly way, remembering, a long, long time ago —
And I was listening to these friends, talking about him,
Because I'd never met him, but I knew who he was,
And at the end of the conversation one of them said to the other
  one,
'Well — and have you heard from him lately?' and our other
  friend said,
'Ah. Well. He's dead just now.' Aye. He's dead just now.

It was here on an island on this side of the world
Quite recently, in fact, and your words were in the air,
On the voices of our children, on the voices of my friends,
Rich in both chuckle and snarl, the most difficult areas:
Teenagers' angst and adults seeing through the shams.
The first calls for laughter, the second for scorn.
What honesty was there, what plenitude of fitting form
And friendliness to all that stays good. Dead just now.
But pass me the book. Let's keep that conversation going.

The High Planes

for Edward Dorn, 1929–1999

      The fury contained in the vessel
injustice breaks in the world
was fierce and vivid, there, within your voice;
but the laughter that assures us
and shreds the opposition,
crackles through the air, anger's light corrective,
redirecting violence, and making accidentalism marvellous.

It was always touch and go
and sometimes, like Yvonne said, when she
started watching *Local Hero*, you see a film beginning
you know you'll never want to end.

Highways, memories of driving at night in Lanarkshire,
red tail-lights swinging back into sight
then away into darkness again, years away
from your long miles of it in all the western sunlight
of 101, one hand tied to the wheel, that poetry
might keep its outlaw status, as all
the best of it does: the sun rests 'deliberately'
on the rim of the horizon. Today's horizon's all
darkening sierra and so long: the hardness of it keeps
your long limbs limber and your shoulders loose, in memory —
the sheer intense propulsion of your gaze, to create —
the opposite of all you'd call indifferent.

'I don't drink whiskey much these days,
but tonight's an exception, now what'll you have?'
When Jennifer suggested you should let me have
a gift to take, another gift, a book —
'He's travelling. He's got to travel light.'
'Well,' she said, 'give him a light book.'
'Well,' you said, 'I could give you *Paterson*.
Now there's a *light* book.'

      Simplicity as honest as
the caustic eye on the old trapeze of money,
Marx and longhorns, the railroads to Chicago
all of us are on, and a rider on the skyline,
seen through the Pullman's curtained window, a moment, now,
crossing the rim, now gone.

Two Paintings by Jack Yeats

A Shop in Sailor Town

and old copper
DEALER IN
OLD IRON

under the sign above the door, under the two yellow oilskins and
  caps, hanging
there, a wee boy jangles pennies in his pocket, looking in
the open doorway, one foot on the threshold. What can there be
in the shop's dark shadowy
interior? His wee pal's standing outside on the pavement, a scarf
around his neck, his head tilted up, he's looking at all he can see
in the window. Their inquisitive backs are facing us. What can
  we see?
Bottles of hair-oil, model ships
in bottles, books, a pistol hanging on a string, a set of knives
hanging on strings, sailors' boots, a painting of a ship in harbour,
two necklaces in a frame, a painting of a beautiful young woman
whose face you cannot see, a big conch shell, a captain's hat,
a flower jar, a box, two watches and beyond these things,
the shadowy dark of the shop's interior.
The two wee boys are standing on the edge of it:
all things new and full of prospect, plenitude and shadows.

Sailor Boy

The sailor boy steps up upon the quay
beside the man with the sickly stare and sickle.
The hour-glass sand is pouring down beside him.
The monkey in the boy's sack over his shoulder is looking at you.
The parrot in the cage he carries cackles.
The rigging creaks. The sounds
of men and women and traffic
from the town across the harbour chime
and tinkle in the filaments of water, lapping
the quay and the tide. The big white clouds blow by.
Some day, even the blue-bright red-striped sailor boy will die.
But for today, the sunlight, stepping ashore, and above, the high
   old sky!

The Boy and the Horse

Two hours driving uphill from Xining,
until the polluted, grey and heavy air of the city
gave way to a place you could breathe in,
and before the next two hours would take us
further uphill, onto the edge of the Tibetan plateau,
through endless fields of bright yellow rapeseed,
past the distant mountains a long way off in the south,
to the edge of Lake Qinghai, a vast pale plane of cerulean,
half-way, therefore, between the crepuscular metropolis
of highrise flats and alleyways and people thronged in markets,
and the silence of the open landscape, the ubiquitous intensity
of sunlight, there on the roof of the world, between
the competitiveness of people and the inhumanity of nature,
in a valley, with the way back down to the city behind us,
and the way on through to the high plains before us,
and mountains and valleys opening on either side of us,
our driver pulled the coach over to the side of the road,
where an open gravel half-circle allowed for
turning, or for watering a thirsty engine, from a hose
coming out of the ground, from a mainline, curved into air
and blossoming water continuously, next to a trough.

The long line of eight coaches was stretched out, each one
stopped along the road and in this lay-by,
allowing a rest for passengers, for some to find relief
beside the trees a little way across the field, and
we sat in our coach quite quietly, just waiting, looking out.

And a boy came riding out of the mountains,
a young man on a horse, just on his own, just that,
in worn grey clothes, and no saddle, simply a rope
from his hands to the head of the horse, riding quite slowly,
out from a valley, into the open half-circle of space
where the bus had pulled up by the side of the road,
and he slowed the horse to a walk as he rode up to the hose
spouting water in a big arcing fountain,
and jumped down and looked at us and wondered.

He watered the horse and looked over his shoulder
at the coaches, the two police-car escort, the people wandering
round from all over the world. And he came slowly up
to the side of our coach and looked at us closely and wondered.
We smiled politely and waved at him gently. He smiled
back at us, beaming, and waved. And then he went back
to his horse, and remounted, and rode back into the mountains.

On the Malvern Hills

And the sky's breath lifted both of them,
the blue, the red, two men in harness, strapped
and corded to their pelmets as the air curved them out,
shields in the azure, quilted with this
substantial occupation: the rising thermal currents
making movement of them, human points
and mechanisms, the sounds as unheard
as the streams appeared invisible, in air.

Like reeds, lifted by the wind, over salt hay
by the river's side, loosened and taken,
spiralled by the rising breath and turned
in lengthening loops and figures, arabesques,
the strain borne even by the hands upon the cords,
the pressures bringing down or over,
out, away to one side or high above
the steeply sloping hillsides, the curving downs below.

On the ridge of the Malvern Hills, David runs ahead,
his seven years of appetite lead quickly to the hill beyond.
Our walking's easy, the pace in the heat of the summery day
unhurried. We crest the second summit, see David now
a tiny figure standing on the third,
shoulders and arms turned back to us
and then — the paragliders cresting the horizon,
sweeping up above him,
sliding down the currents of the col, close to his small shape.

He's looking up at them as they glide by. His breath's intake
I can feel from here — a child whose arms upstretch
to the full moon in the ancient sky, so full of natural want,
for the unattainable.

     — *Windflower*, Elgar called her.
Ah, those rosebud lips. And things all 'wild & headstrong' —
'dreaming of a greatness...by the sedge reeds by the riverside.'
Looking back at the hill-fort of Caractacus, his little army always
facing impossible odds, but standing even now
unchanged on this 'illimitable plain'...
For all the empires of the world have risen to be washed away,
in light-like movement, solid, weighty in the drift of its proximity

     and David's risen gaze —
That unreachable things can be seen
and heard as they move in the air.

5
RIGHT HERE

'It starts with technology but it still ends with tracker dogs.'
RICHARD STARK, *Nobody Runs Forever*

The Eldritch Sprite

after Pushkin

The gurly cludes low'r doun and scowl, blaw
cauld braith, and fling up snaw
in flurries nou. Leanin' oot the windy o' the coach,
I canny hear the horses for its rumblin' —
I canny see the mune, but its sick licht
glisters on the fluchterin' snaw. The nicht is tumblin'
fu' o' static skelfs, like a fuzzy TV screen,
an' in the rowth o' snaw my mind is fleein'
through it a', across the open plain.
The carriage's sma' bells are dingin',
tinklin' in the sworlin' snaw —

'Haud forrit, Driver!'

        'Christ, it's no'
possible, sur. The horses canny dae't' —
slowin' doun tae stumble through
this blizzard's blindin' — *'The road's blocked up —*
I canny see masel'!' —

        An Eldritch Sprite is leadin' us
across the plain and a' aroond this pitmirk nicht
as snaw's confoundin' munelicht —
Haud on. Wheesht nou. The coach slows doun. Bide still a wee.
— And look! Look there! He's there! D'ye see?
Blawin' back an' spittin' at me, playin' —
guidin' the horses inty the gulf

twixt thae twa icy hillocks,
under lowered cludes, wi' gurly braith an' snaw, mair snaw —
The horses like oorsels a' sapped o' strength —
Breathin' steams inside and oot, and watchin' —

'What? Wha's there? What's yon thing there?
A tree-stump or a wolf?'

The snawstorm blaws
The snawstorm blares
The datchie horses snort
His e'en are burnin'
Backward-turnin'
Bleezin' coals in daurk —
Ye see'm nou?

'Driver, Driver, crack'm wi' yir whip!'

An' there he goes —
Leapin' ayont
The laich hills into —
White on black —
A distance only nicht can mak'.

      The horses stert and drive again
The bells ring oot, sma' soundin' in the mirk —
The cludes flee past, the mune I canny see
Lichts up the snaw that flings itsel'
Atween the munelicht's source an' me.
An' deevils wi' their e'en ablaze
Are watchin' frae the slopes wi' skreichy cry
Us, lanely, sluggy, croakily,
As we pass by.

Opening *Hamlet*

after Shakespeare

B.   Wha's there?

F.   Naw, but, answer me. Haud and unfauld yersel'!

B.   Lang live the King!

F.   Barnardo?

B.   Aye!

F.   Fegs, but ye're here oan yir time.

B.   I' th' howe-dumb-deid. Awa' tae yir kip, Francisco.

F.   Mercy tae ye. It's cauld eneuch and I'm richt seek at hert.

B.   Haen ye a quaet guard?

F.   There's no' a moose stirrin'.

B.   Weel, weel. Guid nicht. Gin ye suld see twa ither sauls,
      Tell them — 'Mak' haste!'

F.   I'm thinkin' I'm hearin' them here... Haud! Wha's that?

Enter M. and H.

M.   Freends, freends tae this grund!

H.   Aye, an' leal men tae the Dane!

F.   Aye. Weel, an' guid nicht.

M.   Fareweill, honest sodger. Wha hes yir place?

F.   Barnardo. Guid nicht.

Exit F.

M.   Hoa! Barnardo!

B.   Aye! Is Horatio wi' ye?

H.   Aye, weill, a piece o'm.

B.   Fair fa' an' welcome! Horatio! Marcellus! —

M.   And hes yon thing appeart again the nicht?

B.   I've seen naethin' yet.

M.   Horatio says it's naethin' but oor fantice.
> He'll no' gie ony credit tae the dreidfu' sicht
> We've seen here twice, sae I've brocht him here
> Tae staund attent in the meenits o' this nicht,
> That gin this veesion come,
> He'll grant oor een were true, and speir o't.

H.   Wheesht, wheesht. It'll no' appear.

B.   But nou, sit doun. Gang owre aince mair
> Whit we twa nichts hae witnessed
> Even tae lugs sae stapped as his.

H.   Aye bit sit doun,
> And let us hear Barnardo speak o't.

B.   'Twas juist the nicht afore,
> When yon same star, the west'rt frae the pole
> Had gone its wey tae licht that pert o' heevin
> Whaur it sits bleezin' nou, Marcellus an' masel',
> As the bell struck ane —

Enter GHOST

M.   Wheesht! Oh, wheesht ye nou. Glisk whaur it gangs again!

B.   I' the self-like luik o' the king that's deid.

M.   Horatio, ye're a learnit man — speir at it nou —

B.   Is it no' the king's ain image? Dae ye ken it nou, Horatio?

H.   Maist like. I am dumfoonert a' wi' fear an' wonder.

B.   It begs ye speir o't.

M.   Aye, speir o't, Horatio.

H.   What like are ye, usurper o' this time o' nicht?
          Wi' fair an' warlike form
          The like o' whilk the buried King o' Denmark
          Marched himsel' betimes? Speak! I' Gode's name, speak!

M.   It's taken umbrage.

B.   Luik. It irks awa'.

H.   Haud! Haud! An' speak! —

Exit GHOST

M.   It's gane, an' wullny answer.

B.   Hoo's this, Horatio? Ye trummle an' grow jabbed.
          Is this no' somethin' mair than mere fantice?
          Your thocht, man?

H.   Afore my God, I michtna credit it yet
          Wi'oot the sense an' honest witness
          O' my ain twa een.

M.   Is't no' like the King?

H.   As you are tae yersel'.
          Yon wis the vera armour he hid oan
          When he focht ambitious Norroway.
          An' yince he glowered like that in fushious fecht,
          When strikin' sleddin' Polacks oan the ice.
          It's gey unco'.

M.   An' twice afore, an' juist at this deid 'oor,
          Wi' military sway, he's passed oor watch.

H.   I' what dreid thocht tae work, I canna ken
          But i' the circumspect o' my opeenion,
          It bodes a strange eruption tae oor state.

M.   Aye, weel, sit doon, an' tell me, he that kens,
        Why sic same strict an' maist observin' watch
        Sae nichtly toils the subjects o' the land?
        An' why sic daily cast o' brazen cannon
        An' foreign mart for implements o' war?
        Why sic impress o' shipwrichts, whase sair task
        Pits Sunday i' th' middle o' th' week?
        Whit's up, that sic an sweaty haste
        Suld drive the labour nicht as weel as day?
        Wha can say?

H.   I'll answer ye.
        At least hoo the speik o't is. Oor last king
        Whase image even noo appear't tae us
        Was, as ye ken, by Fortinbras o' Norroway
        Brocht by a jealous pride
        Tae combat. And there oor valiant Hamlet —
        (For sae indeed this hemisphere hes ca'd 'm)
        Slew Fortinbras; wha, by seal'd compact
        Approv't by law and heraldry,
        Norroway'd tae forfeit wi' 'is life
        A' the lands he'd conquer't tae 'is vanquisher.
        An' a moiety King Hamlet tuik.
        An' juist as like wad Fortinbras ha'e ta'en 't a' as his,
        Gin he'd bin vanquisher. But as the thing fell oot,
        His fell tae Hamlet. Nou, sir, young Fortinbras,
        A youngsome, unlearn't, unapproven, gilpy chiel,
        Ran i' the skirts o' Norroway, here an' there,
        Shark'd up a list o' louns wi' fire an' deviltry
        In them. It luiks as like their notion for oor state
        Is to recover what his faither lost, and this, I wad
          jalouse,

Is the drive for a' oor men tae rax an' rive baith day an'
   nicht,
An' brings aboot this rummage in the land.

B.   Aye. Thon's the wey o't.
       It micht yet be that this wanchancy corp
       Gangs through oor watch like the king that wis
       And is the self-same question o' these wars.

H.   A skelf in the mind's ee, makin' it watter:
       In a' the heich an' summery state o' Rome,
       Before the michty Julius Caesar fell,
       The graves were emptied up and a' the deid in windin'
          sheets
       Were gibberin' and squeakin' doon the Roman streets
       Like stern wi' streams o' fire ahint an' bloody dew
       Portend disasters i' th' sun an' moon
       That a' the oceans move by,
       A' seems seek eneuch til Doomsday wi' eclipse.
       An' e'en this foreshadowin' o' evil deeds
       An' prologue to disaster comin' oan,
       Baith Lift and Yird thegither show a'
       Tae a' oor folk and a' their kin and country.

Enter GHOST

       But wheesht, luik there, it comes again!
       I'll beard it, though it blast me. Haud still, ya spook!
       Gin ye've a soond or voice that ye can use,
       Let's hear ye!
       If there is ony guid that I can dae
       That micht gie ease tae you and grace tae me,
       Let's hear o't!
       If ye ken ocht o' this oor country's fate,

Which gin we kent it noo we micht avoid,
Gie voice tae't!
Or gin ye've stashed a secret load in life
O' ill-fared treesure, hid in the wame o' th' yird,
For whilk, deid speerits walk, or so's the speik o't —

THE COCK CROWS

Let's hear o't. Haud nou an' speak. Marcellus, haud it
back.

M.   I'll hack it wi' ma pike —

Exit GHOST

B.   Here it's —
H.   Here it's —
M.   Here. It's awa'.
We do offence, it's o' sic kingly bearin',
To try it oot wi' violence,
For it is as the air, we canny wound it,
An' oor ain vain tries juist mockery.
B.   It wis gaun tae speak when yon cock crew —
H.   An' then it stertit as gin it felt its guilt
An' heard its summons. I've heard
The cock that trumps the morn'
An' waukens up the day, ca's back the deid.
M.   It faded wi' the cock crow in the air.
Fir eftir that, the speerits roam nae mair.
Then nichts are fine an' no ill chance befa's us,
Nor witches dae us hairm.
H.   I've heard the same masel' an' dae believe't.
But luik, the morn is riz in crammassie

Gangs owre the dew o' thon heich eastward brae.
Brak' up nou, an' by my best avisement,
Let's speak o' this we've seen the nicht
Tae Hamlet, the younker, for certes as I breathe,
This speerit, dumb tae us, will speak tae him.
Are we agreed we suld acquent him wi't?
As needfu' in oor lealty, and as fits obeisance?

M.   Let's dae't. Aye. And I this mornin' ken
Whaur we sall find him skulkin' close nearby.

Exeunt

The Weather Log

JESUS: Shall we talk about the weather?
Life is too short, the age is too late
To talk about the weather.
                    EDWIN MORGAN, *AD: The Execution*, Act 1, Scene 2

The dark October streets are washed —
The usual, leaves and rain —
The orange arm of the windmill scythes
slowly through again.

A growling in November midnight
draws us through, to look at the sky —
Turning, angled, circling, at the source of its cone of light,
in the air outside, up high —
Twistily, above Queen's Park, a helicop-
ter — other torches flicker in the trees below, on the hilltop.

Who are they looking for, and why?

The Flying Cloud and the Whale

You lost it. You lost it? How could you lose
a thing that size? Well, he said,
the oceans are bigger
it's easy to lose things, children, crewmen,
ships, whole fleets go missing. What of
a whale? Even a big one, and white, so,
unusual. You shouldn't be able to miss it,
let alone lose it. But you lost it and
went over the side with it when you
found it again, and tried to pin it down.

Well, I lost my whale too. White, equally.
The same guy, in fact, acquired
by purchase, originally, at Arrowhead,
a souvenir, 2 inches long, ceramic or
plaster, left on a white-painted lintel over the doorway
through to the study, at 17A Flynn Road,
a thousand years ago, New Zealand,
when we lived there. We moved. The house
was emptied. Boxes, books, containers, and
one small white whale on the lintel left
behind. But

                    we found it again. When Rae went back
across the wide world, after a long year away,
returned to the house to knock on the door, asked herself in,
went into the corridor, through towards the study, looked up at
  the lintel
and found it again.

So now
it's in Scotland, on top of a bookcase
in another study, sitting just next
to the first airfix model I made with my son,
unbroken in transit, across all the world: *The Flying Cloud*
which, as it happens, my father now tells me,
was the very first model that he ever made, perhaps it would
   have been
the 1940s when he made it for himself
— and now, as it reminds me, leads me on to recollect
my father's Christmas gift to me, sometime in the early 1970s,
the Penguin *Moby-Dick*, edited by Harold Beaver (I heard him
   lecture once,
at Cambridge) and the breath left my body when Ahab went over
   the side.
— *The Flying Cloud* and Moby-Dick, pretty much to scale,
on top of that wooden bookcase in the study, three corners away
from Mr Burns's house, in Alloway.

The Banks Business

On the crossing, on the ferry, I read *The Business* by Iain Banks.
Having read it, and having it in my hand
on the helicopter deck of the *Port of Bilbao*,
I was seized by the impulse to hurl it into the Bay of Biscay, which,
a nearby notice about whales and how to spot them informed us,
is over 3,000 metres deep in places.

This impulse was creative,
rather than critical.
I was suddenly taken by the image:
The neat, dry density of words — to be hand-held,
to be read in the light — suddenly spun out above the sea
— the ocean — to look for an instant like a badly designed seagull,
   flapping
its white covers like disabled wings. Then the splash,
the thirst of dry pages for water. The black and white of its
   design
in the wash of the ship's wake...
Into my mind came scraps of Phlebas,
The Tempest, Byron. They bob about and sink.

Once, at the age of about nine, during a summer holiday,
I found myself standing, as I often would, at the quay's edge in
    Tarbert.
My hand was in my pocket, jingling pennies.
That seizure of impulse.
I took one out and flipped it away, down to the deep-green slick
    of the harbour water.
It winked and winked beautifully, catching the sun
until at last it just
disappeared, disappearing
beautifully, too.
I repeated the process with the other coins in my pocket.

A month or so later, back at school,
I was called to the front of the class.
My act had been observed.
I was held up now as a salutary example of some kind of badness —
mainly betrayal
of that cardinal virtue,
'thrift'.

I still have the novel.
It is now neatly shelved
with the other Bankses
with their matching black and white design.

A lesson to us all,
that there are always those
who seek to arrange their evil publicly,
on the innocent shelves of the minds of children.

Killing the Rat

Glen's eyes narrowed, he breathed
smoke to one side, his fingers
protective of
the cigarette, nervous: 'I hate them,'
he said, knowing what was there,
behind that tall green door.

The high brick building was The Stables, and
thirty years ago it had been that, but now Glen used it
for storage, for big cardboard boxes of eggs. He brought them in
by van, from the batteries and farms,
delivered them to shops and factory canteens.
And tonight, in the gathering dusk, in the yard outside
the closed green door, he was thinking of the rat that had got in.

We went in. I was ten, eleven, maybe twelve.
'Stand there,' he said. I waited by the door, closed now
as quick as we entered. All around, in the tall cold air,
the cardboard boxes were piled high,
different sizes of eggs inside them noted
by different coloured printing on the sides.
As boys, we climbed among them, played
hide-and-seek, but not tonight. I was there
to watch. Could I help? 'Just stand there,' he said,
and started to move.

He took the wooden pole from a broom-head
and crouching, quickly moved
to the boxes stacked by the wall on the right,
pushed the pole down between the boxes and the wall,
and rattled it.
                  We heard the rustle.
The scrut, patter, tensile bitter whisper
of something that wanted to eat or kill or escape.
It moved behind the boxes, scraped
along the wall.

Glen moved away, walked quickly
to the stacks of boxes piled beside the wall
in front of us, leant down and grasped
the cut-away grip of handle on the lowest one, and pulled it out
six inches from the wall. The height and weight
kept all the boxes stacked and firm in place above it,
only this one on the concrete floor stuck out
to that extent, but all above and there
on either side, closed up and tight and neat,
and heavy, full of eggs.

            Every stack was out about an inch,
from each of these three walls: to our right,
to our left, and ahead of us. Behind us was the fourth wall and
the closed door. Behind the stacked boxes on the right,
the rat.
            The snare was set.

Glen moved like a man afraid, and swallowing
his fear, to act like a man of courage, to get this done.
Knowing that to leave it as it was, would bring more in,
and that a fight like this would turn the thing
to frenzy and an unpredicted leap, a bite, a scratch,
might leave disease or a wound unclean and painful.
He started to move with intent.
      He must have known that all I had to do
was stand where I was and watch, and act as I would
when I had to, which was only what one would
do, anyway.
      He moved fast now, rattling the pole
in the space where he'd been before, then out to the front
of the boxes, bringing the pole against the outer wall of them
with a *crack!* out loud on the concrete floor and a *crack!* again
  crack!
And the rat, you could hear it,
               starting to move
behind the boxes, fast then faster, down that
side of the wall on the right to the corner,
sharp left, then fast
along the back wall in front of us —
crack! crack! crack!
and along the back wall to the left, then up
the left wall to the edge of the boxes, the end
of the stacks, and Glen running after it,
cracking the pole on the concrete again and again and shouting
as he was running, and then
             it appeared
out from behind the boxes, as hard

and vicious in its look and its narrowing
appraisal of the scene. For a moment,
it stopped and stared.

I'd turned and stared at it, and Glen
had reached it with his pole and struck at it, and turned
it back, and back it went, now faster
back, down the left wall, sharp
turn right, along the back wall, sharp
turn right, and up the right wall, and as Glen
chased after it, racing it up to a frenzy, and
it appeared again there, where the stacks stopped
on my right. And this time as Glen
moved to chase it back in, I joined in, stepping
forward, waving my arms and shouting, and *crack!*
it was gone again racing and much faster now,
knowing, perhaps, all exits were blocked, but
not knowing, now, Glen cracked the pole
one more time then dropped it, ran
in a sprint as fast as the rat and faster and threw
himself forward,
feet first now, hitting and sliding along
on the flat concrete floor on his back,
crossing that last short distance and judging,
at speed, the sheer acceleration
and velocity, his body-weight, and that
of the rat, as it whipped round that back wall,
reaching almost half-way
as Glen's moving feet and his torso propelled
them to hit square-on the box he'd pulled out

that deadly six inches and now
smashed back in,
          crushing the rat as it ran
between the boxes and the back wall, bringing
the boxes into alignment again.
We heard the black crunch of its bones.

Glen pulled himself up from the floor.
We waited in silence, waiting for sounds
of any kind. Nothing.

And we're back outside,
in the back yard, and the dusk has turned
to sunset: there's a red sky over there, above
the outside wall by the fields beyond The Stables,
and the backyard lamp on the roof is phosphorescent yellow in
approaching midnight blue, star-needlepointed sky.
Glen has the dead rat carried
on a square of cardboard, torn
from an egg-box, held like a tray in his hand,
and in one turning, sweeping gesture sure, all
his body registers revulsion and rejection as he
swings and dips and raises, arcs and throws
in a great, disparaging trajectory,
the dead rat, into the night.

The Review
or, 'I won't facilitate Vicki today'

a poem with five footnotes

Dire was his thought, who first in poison steep'd
The weapon form'd for slaughter — direr his,
And worthier of damnation, who instill'd
The mortal venom in the social cup,
To fill the veins with death instead of life.

WALTER SCOTT, Rob Roy

You're going to undergo
a review of yourself. It's like,
make a small clone, on a petri dish,
but don't grow the head
or the limbs or the torso.[1]
You're going to write a
'self-evaluation document'
which will openly disclose your strengths...
and weaknesses. Especially helpful will be,
those places, chinks they might be,
through which can be detected
'room for improvement'...
Well,
thus it ever was: you have
'room for improvement' until you achieve
'optimum enhancement capacity'[2]
(i.e., you're dead)

'Look on it as an opportunity.'[3]

— *But I don't want*
a nostrum for every faculty…

And faculties work better
Free, but not directionless,
when the directives are supplied
not by nostra[4]
but *created* by the dynamics provided
by the company (call it an
assembly, call it a collective) of
people related by subject, commitment and place.
And — and here's the rub —
by the prevalent attitude to experience.[5]

1   It's not for dancing with, or thinking.
2   Otherwise, 'maximum facilitation potential'.
3   Keeps someone in work. Worms gotta eat too.
4   In fashion or otherwise, the old ones are still the best: brute force or dis-
     employment, whatever it is intimidates to purpose.
5   Turn on the TV and go to work.

Two Corryvreckan Poems

for Peggy and Glen Murray

1   *The Element*

A flight of dolphins shoaling by
as if it were not sea but sky.

A Minke's tall black curving fin
slides anti-clockwise, right back in.

Two shearwaters skate the air
wings as sharp as fins right there.

And up the sound of Jura in Force 7, the ketch and bodies angled
in water that makes light, vision, muscle, tense, taut, tangled.

Purpose, gauge, the strength of will, urgency, resolve and love
of all that matters, takes us, finally, carefully, cautiously, moored,
    by rope and chain, both fore and aft, into that soft cove.

At anchor, the curious seals rise now and then and keek,
their rounded heads are bullet points that punctuate the week.

2   *At Tobermory*

The ripped sail needs patching.
Needle and thread.
        Held taut
as the strong hands direct, point and draw.
A criss-cross of hatchings contract and connect.
It will hold, and the sail keep its belly
when filled.

        Needle and thread:
returning to the harbourfront,
the narrow streets and closes traced behind it —
my father's childhood haunts —
the tree-filled hills rise up beyond the curve of bay, the row
of brightly-coloured shops, hotels and bars, the pier —
pausing once or twice to say hello
to older friends from long ago.

Then back to the sea once again.

— Held taut, the mind will point and draw.
The thread cross-hatched and holding.

Vanishing Point

And here in far Tiree, the scattered houses smiling at each other,
we drive along the roads, recirculating, letting acquaintance deepen.
The white school bus swings over the road on the curving horizon
   behind us,
looms up into our mirrors. And so, with slowing courtesy,
we pull into the passing place and wait for him to overtake
with a modest, friendly wave for acknowledgement.
And the bus drives on, over the gentle curves ahead of us.
Mid-afternoon and this school day has ended.

The houses in their isolated places have fewer, smaller windows
than you might think. They all look out at distances in air and
   land,
to sea. Three fields further on, and the road slows down again,
the school bus coming back. Over on the far left field,
a tall young boy swings satchel from its straps across his shoulder,
skylined as he strides uphill to home, and spares us only a glance.
There are two figures up at the house, and washing on the line.

The breeze picks up and brushes out the hair
of two girls walking towards us by the roadside,
and up on a platform of scaffolding, two men in blue dungaree
   overalls
are working on a roof, repairing beams. I lift my hand and one
   waves
back with a smile, his hand and his mouth scarcely moving.
A minimal act, but there to be seen and noted,
on the human side of the vanishing point.

Thieves

Don't be deceived. That white sand crushed shell beach
Is beautiful, no doubt. The Technicolor turquoise sea
And great white foambelled waves,
The freshly laundered dunes and brightly waving machair
Are beckoning. But.
The water is ice. The machair cuts the townie's soft bare feet.
And not that beach, but the next one round the coast,
Is quicksand, silently sucked down a man
Some years ago, still in living memory.
It's an unreliable landscape. Not
What it looks like at first glance.
Its emptiness has been produced by others,
And those who remain are either long-standing residents,
Scratching what they can from the crofts, or incomers
Who can afford their own holiday homes. Fine for them.
But it is not the populated landscape
Where a people with a language made to match
Can live in their own dynamics, create an economy sustaining
All the arts and conversation.
All of it is edged, beyond the mass appeal of snapshot pictures.
The great writers of these places, Gaelic poets
Like Mary MacLeod, and Derick Thomson,
And poets in the English language too, Iain Crichton Smith
And Norman MacCaig: these landscapes are named
In their poems. But none
Of these landscapes name their poets.
There are no plaques on walls or maps to show
Identities of language and religion, beliefs and faiths

And what convictions are.
A shop displays more local books by ministers
Than work by any of the poets
Named above. It is not good enough.
We are thieves of our own best destiny,
Denying what our arts can do.
We want bare walls and silence. No paintings.
No poems. No idolatry. No iconography.
The beautiful bare beaches that
Cover up a life
As silently as that.

Luskentyre at twilight.

Flat sand, flat sea, extending all that way.
And wind moving laterally,
Rippling the water,
    Millions of tiny ribs of water. Millions of them, extending
Over the sand, and suddenly
                    In the twilight, my eyes adjusting, slowly,
That delicacy, as driving past on the narrow road, and passing
(Uncle Mac driving the big Mercedes, his eyes on the road)
The weight of all that history —
MacCaig's great poem, 'Aunt Julia'
I've been teaching now for more than twenty years, loving it,
And suddenly I'm surprised by the sight
Of the cemetery —
        The sandy graves at Luskentyre —
And the loss, through thievery,
Of language and the people from it, and more —
What is lost from the world even now as we see it again —

And sometimes we deny ourselves for very good reason indeed,
Living with a little regret.
The following morning,
I am walking towards the glass door of the building in the town,
  in Tarbert,
Next the tourist information office,
And walking towards it from the other side,
A woman I knew from a long time ago, twenty years maybe,
And our eyes catch each other with such speed,
Recognition and decision almost simultaneous,
To pass each other silently, like that.

Like thieves, stealing from history
All that might have been
For the benefit of all there is, the good of it.

A brightness, of a kind.
And an ambiguity.

Madness

Their virtue was to see
That an expanding economy
Was not a good thing. The economy should serve
The quality of life, and when they were offered the chance
Of 'improvement'
They flatly denied the rich man's proposition.
Leverhume, leave us alone.
The problem is, that insight into the value of such quality
Is vulnerable. When should turns to must.
A simple religious belief
In independent thought takes on
A massively twisted weight when it becomes
An absolute. The counter-Reformation
Comes out of the same Big Bang
As the Reformation, pilgrims.
And this is what you get:

The hotelier opens the door of the bar on a Sunday
And in comes the letter, of course
The back door would be permissible
But please observe the preference, and keep the front door closed.
And she says No in thunder. To be preached against from all
The pulpits in the long, long island, and still
To live there, not surrendering
To the hypocrisy.

The churches are terrifying and comical.
Their conversions of children are brutal and pathetic,
Like the little people, like Hitler. Killing
By generations. Or those who make us laugh, like Chaplin,
Reminding us of our absurdity, being human
As we are. Reminding us, what dignity is. Not this.

Truly such monstrous perversion
Must be admired for its strangeness.

We were driving past a funeral at Scarista.
There was a certain dignity indeed,
All those men in black
Standing up at the house.
There also was a frightening absurdity
In all the empty cars parked by the roadside, more than a
  hundred,
Bumper to bumper, nose to tail, all along the road. All sorts,
Parked as they were, against a big backdrop of sun, sand and sea.
You had to think, Godard, or Bergman meets Lynch.
Or Beckett, at the very least.

The best people to work with are those who share your laughter
And for whom you always keep some respect. Piety won't do.
The mafia preserve the terrible judgement of faith,
So let us remember how laughter enacts
The lasting conspiracies of value.
Let's cultivate the usefully derisive height. Ask questions. Be
Sceptical. Be cynical, professionally, cold. Forensic.
The facts are plain enough. Don't let the madness rule.

But it does. So many, again and again, so far, so deep,
So do the churches move, across the generations. The absolutes.
The closed. In total contradiction of the democratic voices raised
In singing of the Psalms, the long tunes, the seafaring sounds.
Lord, I am not going forward. The cuiram is a madness, Lord.
Lord, I am not going forward. Oh Uncle Mac, keep driving!
Here comes another church. Duck!

Orkney Postcards

February 2007

1   The Gloup

Fifty minutes snatched from schedules took us to
an openness of sky, sea, out-stretched headlands
and the pleasure of the short walk to the Gloup.
       — 'I don't know what road we're on.
       Where would you like to go?' (handing over
       the map) 'To the moon!' Of course.
The Gloup was good enough. A tiny silver burn
streams down the pathside, suddenly becomes
a fall beneath our feet, the wooden platform
inches from the great stone gulf there, opening
before us: the sea reaching in, reaching up
the walls of stone through a gap in the cliffs,
tidal, remindingly recurrent, the great big tug —
the world is out there, and there's this:
a moment's friendly sense that's shared,
about what's vulnerable, worth keeping hold of, opening out.

2   The Ring-Tailed Lemurs in Galloway
(*'opening out...'*)

'Which leads me on to tell for sport...'
as Burns once wrote, as carelessly (it seemed) as I will now,
about the wildlife park in Galloway. The keepers caged
the ring-tailed lemurs, running back and forth

on branches, down long criss-crossed metal fencing, or
through wide zig-zags of corridors. They'd tried them in
the open air, but they clustered in camp, in shelter,
shy. So fencing made them happy and they
scampered up and down. But the keepers have a plan.
As months turn into years, one said, they'll take the fencing down,
open up the rooftops of the cages, let them loup
to the trees, and as a generation passes on
its skills and limits to another, hope to see a greater freedom
come without anxiety, upon them. Out from the south
of Scotland, the ring-tailed lemurs will roam!
Survivors from an ancient past, to live as wild as
native creatures will, with families extending, all the way to Orkney.

3   At Eric Linklater's Grave

At Merkister Hotel, on Harray Loch, the water's lively,
blustery wind streams through across the carpark. 'Up the hill,'
the hotel owner tells me, 'That's St Michael's Kirk.
That's where he's buried. Marjorie too, beside him.
You'll find them: they're there like standing stones.'
Sure enough, on the crest of the wind-blasted hill,
my hair and jacket and trousers flapping like flags,
and all the blue bays and green fields before me,
that's where they are. A ragged stone for him, a finger pointing up.
A diagonal line for her stone, leaning towards him.
'Praise be to God' beneath his name. A little way off,
I see an apple on the grass, one of those you find
painted bright red, for show in shop windows. This one's white,

the bright enamel all washed off. I pick it up, remembering
the words in *Magnus Merriman* (who else wrote like this?):
Her bra lay on the carpet like 'grapeskins discarded on the rim of
  a plate'.
And I settle the styrofoam apple by his headstone, out of the wind,
and breathe: 'Praise be to Him indeed, but give the Devil his due.'

4   Wyre and the Bu

'Out of this desolation we were born...'
But that was Edwin Muir and clapping psalms
that shivered out the ebb-tide far too far
till nothing seemed returning but a dream of sunny holms,
of fabled horses and — a childhood full of summer.
Today the wind is flattening, the paths' mud
ankle-deep, the fences barbed or wired with shock
for straying sheep or cattle, Muir's father's farm
cold grey in early February light, the road
a running line on time, affording views of islands levelled,
all heights blown down and polished to
their lowly curves and pieties; the wreckage
of a vision, both lovely and unreal.
Returning to the ferry, *Eynhallow*, I'm caught by a man
on the skyline: his cap secure, his shoulders square,
his jacket blown out against clouds.
He's walking, steady, out across the daybreak,
scattering seed. I look again: There are the planted rows.
There is a crop. The mud and water squelches through
my shoes and socks. I walk and clench my toes.

5   *Threaded on Time*

Driving after dark through Hamnavoe at a snail's pace,
manoeuvring the narrow winding main street, past empty
close-mouths, alleyways, voes running down to the sea
where the sea's running up: this tidal little town, on waterfront
and hillslope, steep thin streams murmuring descent.
Ferry, ocean, travellers, return upon their different tides and seasons.
And I. 1976: That long summer's exploration landed me,
one afternoon, with GMB, after a flurry of letters,
this long conversation, as the gift of a salmon arrived,
and knowledge of the hesitancy needed in this given world,
added to by his kind words supporting. Then 1995:
and me a married man, and GMB again that afternoon,
slowly recollecting, piece by piece: 'That salmon, yes,
and you were here with someone, then... But now I'm fallen
"into the sere and yellow"...' Now, 2007: a blue plaque
on the wall. That's good. And on a sunny, windswept afternoon,
there's Warbeth spread before me like a harbour or a comfy bed
new-made. Beside his Mum and Dad, but with the adult words
   he made,
around his stone: a silence to be content in. The salt is in the air.

6   *Validation*

The work we did — to read through all the documents
concerned to make it real: an Arts degree, a programme
in 'The Literature of Highlands and Islands' — exhausted us
and all of us were thorough; but the sense that this was needed

here and should be needed here was all-important as we worked
the details through. The following day, I met a man, a solitary one,
who told me he had moved his life from England.
His thin, fractured sentences came haltingly and forced.
He'd been bullied at school and suffering came through a life
unhelped by learning, art or share of grace. But always, he said,
he'd had this sense, of wanting to live in Scotland, in the far north,
in these islands. Now, he'd sold all he had in the south. He was
working hard on a run-down house on an island of eighteen people,
to try to make it worthwhile. When I told him my name, he
stopped, gasped, gaped, stared: his cousins, he said, were named
as me. And his name? When he told me, was as good a Scottish
name as any. 'But — my family's English,' he said.
'They've always lived near Huddersfield. I never knew
there was anything Scots about it.' We paused on that.
'Well,' I said. 'They must have come from somewhere.'

7   Drawn back by magic

Whatever the hand holds: camera, paintbrush, pencil, pen
the fingertips upon the laptop's keys, the paper, screen or canvas
and the air the senses carry in — make traces, tracks, a patterning
that moves out from the place and its location on the clock,
to be caught, glimpsed, held on, whatever may be,
and at whatever time, but never trapped. That is what work we do,
what help it might be, crosses then to now;
but it is not only that. It also brings you back. Something unplanned,
intuitive, relaxed, working in the bones and muscle,
way below the memory of things: abstraction, yet as real
as that salt spray that hit you like a shower switched on

when the ferry smashed the cross-wave and a blast
of blue and green turned white as frost and drenched
you in a sudden cold — as if all resolution, steel and ice
were sensitised. Or that moment in Kirkwall Cathedral,
writing in the book: the third time now, to see in Orkney,
what has changed and what remains, and by whatever
chance and will should be, what's drawn back by magic.

Elgar in Scotland

1   *Prelude, early 1880s*
(Solo cello)

I've crossed this border more than once
but what do borders mean? We have an Empire.
Borders form at the precipice, narrow valleys cross them,
rivers. And rivers make borders as well, like, Solway to Tweed.
I crossed this border first with Dr Buck. Charles Buck.
We were on holiday, in the Lakes, went wandering
north. My music, his surgery. It's all medicine.
His work crosses borders of the body, as does
mine, affecting the rhythms and pulse of
the interior, to help what life there is. Diagnostic. Remedial.
The hope of a cure. Who's to say we have not more
in common, than apart? The art and science of
unmapped terrain, imagination's large geography,
the lonely work of bringing it to bear.
But membranes are required, like skin.
Good walls are built to keep things out and in.
And let them pass, the cochlea. At first,
one is silent before them. That teaches respect.
The long stone line of Hadrian's wall —
                    sweeps and curves and rises and leans
laterally all along this border, as the pathway
does the same, along
                   the ridge of the Malvern Hills.
Except...

Except the Roman wall divides us.
What carries across? Birdsong. Birds. The clouds
and sounds in air. But not forever, distances insist.
Some voices are resisted, others welcome.

2 *Travelling in the North, 1884*
(*An Encounter*)

Helen was the first, most welcome, love, now gone
to the furthest place the great globe's diametrics point to:
New Zealand. There is no holding on across such distances.
That's a border, crossed. I'll never hear her voice again.
Helen was a Protestant. I am Roman Catholic.
There are some things, I do believe, require our deep assent.
Questions are impertinent, absurd. Prayer has a value for spirit,
to start from a listening silence. That is more
than resistance, when all resistance is
is habit, vanity, too much sound, cacophony. No need for that.
But now no company beside me, either. And always need for that.
Last time, Charles and I, we ventured no great journey.
This time I'm alone. I shall go north, and far.

Glasgow. Alone, depressed.
            'Dear Dr Buck,
A very desponding state (you ken
what happened). The Continent was closed to me,
so I thought of Scotland.'
            To Rothesay, Ardrishaig and Oban,
Monday the 11th of August. Out round Mull and Staffa.
Mendelssohn's Cave. Can't get that out of my head.

Ballachulish. Through Glencoe. These placenames are
their own terrain and echo. What do we remember by them?
How far do they call up things that lie around us, what they mean?
The past is what we hear and see right now.
The place embodies it, literally.
The way the people live here.

I needed to clear my head.
These are not my landscapes nor my people but
they tell me clearly what I need to do,
what best to do with everything I've learnt. So,
no more the little band at the asylum. I shall compose.

Lonely as one would be,
I was looking out and listening, and heard:
a new voice that attracted me at once.

I met her on the boat upon Loch Etive, sailed with her
to Corpach. No-one will know her now. We laughed.
She laughed on, eyes caught. Prettily, with strength in all that
landscape, loch-scape, movement, momentary
friendship made by a passing remark, a gesture
none could foresee, a deference, politeness, a risk,
ventured, given, responsiveness, a musical offering,
concurrence of initials. 'Let's meet again,'
I said. 'In Inverness.'
                    Next day she was with tourists,
I passed through Fort Augustus, hearing
the bells from the priory, noted their tune
in my diary. Got to Inverness, to the Station Hotel.
We met once again.

You ask what she was like, compared to Helen.
How does love compare? What makes one less
or more or lasting or what time allows of it
to enter us, across the borders we set up,
despite ourselves, resisting it?
We each tasted whisky together, a little,
and breathed it gently, a pleasure shared.

On Sunday I found the Catholic church,
then went to the islands again.
South in Inverary, the Protestant free kirk.
They have their music too.
I noted down a hymn tune, kept it carefully. The difference is,
You are yourself a solitary church. There is some truth in that.
No company can help this loneliness. And even here,
This simple, strong-souled hymn tune tells of it.

Her name began with letters as did mine:
as I shall write, elaborate enigmas.

I stayed on alone in Inverness and planned to meet her once again,
in Edinburgh. On Thursday, the 21st of August, we did,
and visited the Palace
of Holyrood House, the National Gallery,
heard the Scots Guards play.
The fun of it! and then, we parted: Friday, August 22nd.
Never to see her again.

Back to Glasgow then. South again to Worcester. England. Home.

You ask me what became of it —

Well, there was 'An Idyll' (the number 1 of opus 4)
published the following year, and dedicait: to 'E.E., Inverness' —
A clarity. A pleasure. An immediacy danced, a partner
touched, and then let go. A border crossed, recrossed in patterns,
movements, time that goes in more than one direction,
when you hear it clearly —

        Of course I came back, but scrapped
the fragments of what might have been —
the Scottish Overture was started then
but English William Stockley said
it sounded 'disconnected'. He
did not conduct it in Birmingham.
I think he was afraid of it.

Whose loss are things we cannot hear?
What shall survive of us? What's needed
most, by those we can't foresee?
What voices even now will we hear yet?
What sounds of streams and trees, of wind upon the hills?
And who will then hear us, in places that we can't foretell,
by virtue of technologies we cannot now predict?
What purpose brings to life again
the motives, words and music we have made?
        The dead, the dear departed,
are in another place. Latterly, I heard
my music through a new machine.
Imagination makes things, helps us see
how things might be, outside of linearity.
The needle drops in on a gramophone record.
The symphony has its arc too, its solitary life, trajectory.
But any given moment is a texture of connection, simultaneity,

borders woven in, together, unravelling in time. She is there.
And Helen is there. And they are there too —
All that was then to come: dream children, horses, in time.

3 *At Inverness, 1884*
   (*Reflections*)

What songs they have in Scotland! What music!
Not English songs at all. Vaughan Williams will come after me
and tune himself in to Elizabethan idylls, choral imperial dreams.
Larks ascend to thinning air and vanish in the sky.
But I want the whole symphonic tradition behind me.
I shall assume and command it.
The orchestra is complex and diverse.
A multitude of voices in expression and desire.
I want to hear all of those voices, in
a mutual respect, a world of different sounds.
The movements certain, cellos, something charged
beyond the words the human voice can say. That's it.
Something beyond words, that carries a sense
of its own loneliness.
          The grandeur lies in the loneliness,
not in the march and the martial, but
the pathos of the epic effort —
          something in the space
in the space where God was.
And I have the sense of it here.

When I crossed the border, nothing happened.
Oh I know, of course, the sign you say exhilarates,
deep breaths of that fresh air, the carriage window down.
But no. The train rolled on. The smoke rolled by. The soot
stained my fingers and the pages of my book.
But when I reached the North, and knew it was the North,
the air indeed was different. Something happened.
The space you could be lonely in was open.
I was outside every day, walking, fishing, climbing in the hills,
occupying air, with all my tumbling mind could give to it.

Later, I would write it all. The urgency of flesh
that needed company, of mind that needed
dedication, arts of self-determining, imagination's
work. These things at this distance, now,
begin to show so clearly.
Now, some more compelling force
of circumstance, design, desire, and moment,
makes a crystal, polyhedron,
opening and indicating, forward.

4   *At Aberdeen, 1906*
    (*Brass band; then solo clarinet*)

What happened next was different.
Pomp, of course. And circumstance.
The rising tide of Britishness had come
as far as Aberdeen. Marriage, reputation,
knighthood and the night train north,
the cold east coast, the warmth of the reception,

King and Queen and Lord Strathcona, Andrew Carnegie,
The Archbishop of Canterbury, and all of the eminent guests,
at Marischall College, where I was happily given
the LLD degree, honorary (free)
and stayed with Sanford Terry, out in Cults.

Far from alone is loneliness as well.
At 'Westerton of Pitfodels' we talked of Bach,
and played. What passion swells the numbers!
What other mathematics gives such ocean depths?

Scott confirmed my sense of human decency
Not 'pompous chivalry' for all that stuff,
But simply civil manners and good heart.
Froissart — breathe it hushed — I got from *Old Mortality*.
The 'big bow wow'? I think not. He knew as well as I —

What tides rise up and fall, in time!
What's drowned in all the blood my body carries?
My memory, the tenderness with which
I touch this crystal glass,
                    my wife's pale skin,
the vulnerable things
            no pomp and circumstance
protects?
            No ceremony stills
The beating heart, the solitary body
Standing here, at night,

looking out at what was yet to come.

5 *At the Gairloch Hotel, 1914*
(*Trio: cello, piano, violin*)

We journeyed on the 19th of July.
Carice was just a girl, and scared,
the precipice beside us, the driver leaning, 'slightly drunk'
and swaying over the horses. So what was I to do
but smile at her and bring her voice to join mine,
singing nonsense songs, for fun? We knew
a good repertoire, but my eyes went over her head
to Loch Maree, that shining splendour still,
the carriage rolling on, the cliffs below on one side,
the rising rock encroaching on the other.

At the hotel, you can look out
across all Gairloch Bay, over the Minches to Skye
and even, far-off, Lewis.

'The wild birds feed their young
within 30 yards of this window —
gannets, oyster-catchers and divers
and a dozen others.'

Alice said she thought it was 'the loveliest place' —
ever. Except Bavaria, of course.
Carice and I went fishing. Alice didn't.

The 4th of August came. The idyll ended.
The guests began to leave. One old couple stayed,
and us. Breakfasts were all crockery,
and cutlery, and heaviness of linen.

I couldn't get the news.
No papers. Post disrupted.
Car drivers gone with their cars.
The steamer had been taken to the islands,
to pick up men for soldiering. The hotel coaches,
broken down, awaited parts from Glasgow.
The locals refused my English £5 notes.

It was 'weird and affecting' seeing these things,
'those dear people bidding goodbye'
       '...the Lovat Scouts rode thro
— were given a sort of tea meal here
& rode off in the moonlight by the side of the loch
& disappeared into the mountain.'

Next day, Achnasheen, and Inverness again,
and Perth and Edinburgh, then back to the south,
vast movements of men to be seen on the way.

The troop trains passing through on their way to the south —
Much further south than England.
Already there was sorrow.
The end of *The Apostles*. No more oratorios.
Not 'God be thanked' but whispers, *Sospiri*.

All was strangely soundless, as if it were a silent film —

Later I dreamt, of course —

6　*The Dream*, 1914
(*String Quartet*)

The sounds of iron, horses' hooves —
The clattering on cobbles, young men in the moonlight —
Hundreds and hundreds of young men on horses —
Clean pale blue jaws and officers with big moustaches,
Gloved hands on the reins,
Holding them high. The sounds of horses snorting,
Riding through together,
Solennelle, en masse, a thick moving column riding past the hotel —
I stood on the veranda, watching them go,
The curve of the column, riding —
　　　　　　　　The water crashing in on the beach down below
The far loch glittering and still, the high craggy mountains
　behind us —
And dream-like into the twilight of dawn creeping up, they rode
Into the rising road that would take them —
The men and the horses, into the dark,
As the dawn brought slowly its chorus
of birdsong, the accents of silence,
the voices, again, of women and men,
and the absence —

The absences —

The loss of things to come —

7   *In Oban, 1924*
(Solo cello, then solo piano)

I am alone again. Alice has been dead four years.
When you do love and live with one so dearly, so close
your trust becomes connected over year upon year,
whatever the absences are, the gulfs. The taste of breakfast
marmalade, the avatar of fragrance, roses,
or lavender. As simple as that.
What we have is common and shared
because we are separate, strengths beyond fragility,
creating something once again, reliable.
Across borders.
But vulnerable things live on, the sensitive persists.
Friends, there are many, now, who share in the smile, are grateful for
the humour. None who know the structures of support
that intimacy brought, the trust
that meant equality,
before the God all works at last present themselves
as human creatures do.

It is August. It is Oban. It is raining
again. Incessant mist and cold.
It suits me at this 'lonely, meditative end
of life.'
            And yet, perhaps,
To Shetland and St Kilda…?

'Dear Windflower,
      This desolation suits me now
I came here forty years ago alone.
I have had my career. There's a difference.
Then I was unknown. Now I go into the Bank
of Scotland and they cash my cheque at once.
I call that fame, in Scotland!'

I am not sure, where next, but
Sometime in the month ahead
I shall go back to Inverness,
Back to the Station Hotel.
Where else should I go? Except...
Except, the place called remembering.

For as certain as I am that I am here now,
so you shall hear me once again, 'someday...'

Mission Impossible:
Sherlock Holmes and Dr Watson

Digital technology makes possible the recreation of moving
images from photographs of the dead. This allows a
magical film to be made telling the story of Sherlock
Holmes and Dr Watson. They are played impeccably
by Norman MacCaig and Sorley MacLean.
MacCaig as Holmes is tall, lean, high-cheekboned, a little
grey and tweedy in dress, quite spartan in comforts,
intellectually self-sufficient but with a substantial personal
library servicing his own esoteric and obsessive interests.
He is determined in concentration and absolutely certain
in his modes of analysis. His conclusions are reliable but
somewhat repetitive. He plays the fiddle but knows his
limits. He requires a regularly self-administered drug,
referring to the glass as 'the needle'. He is an expert on ash.
MacLean as Watson is much more rough-hewn, hard-headed and
serious-minded than his popular film image. He has known
tragedy in love. He carries a wound from an old war in the
east. He has an unpersuadable commitment to matters of
human value and social worth. When they go into action,
he carries the gun.
Both share senses of humour, generosities of spirit, depths
of compassion and understanding, severities of belief.
Occasionally, individually or mutually, their eyes will
twinkle and gleam with recognitions.
They are called upon to investigate land-rent frauds, duplicitous

government organisations, irresponsible authorities, cruel and twisted religions, violent crimes against the people and the hidden nature of reality.

In the end, the disguise of London is cast off and the city is revealed as Edinburgh. The Reichenbach Falls are in Sutherlandshire.

Moriarty is Henry Dundas.

A different kind of technology (developed after fully-funded research into literary tonalities conducted through intuitive methodology by wise and experienced practitioners) makes it possible to confirm that the film would be approved by MacCaig, MacLean and Arthur Conan Doyle.

The film is immediately judged brilliant and increasingly loved by generation after generation.

It wins Oscars for all concerned. Recognising that the only democratic way to deal with a monopoly of power is absolute constructive devolution, the US Government makes large sums of money available to support a major film industry in Scotland.

Some of the money is used to turn McCaig's Folly in Oban into a Centre for Poetry, Film and the Performing Arts, with satellite links to all the world.

The Excuse

It's one of those eerie, silent nights
when the snowfall's so heavy the buses are off
and the traffic's down to zero, almost. Uncle Mac gets through.
He parks the big Mercedes in Sauchiehall Street, rather than
    attempt
the steep slope up to Garnethill, to go to John & Yvonne's
for dinner. Afterwards, he's walking back
and sees the group of three or four, well-dressed
and frolicsome, young men out from a restaurant
and dodging around the car. One
sweeps his hand across the bonnet, ducks
as a white bomb whistles past his head,
lets fly himself. Mac presses the alarm release on the key ring,
the lights flash orange twice, the man is stopped, midway
through gathering more snow off the Merc's big bonnet, glances
round, sees Mac, grins, and shrugs: 'Sorry, pal —
I was trying for a better class of snowball.'

The Answer

'We must be patient,' I said. 'What we wait for now is the fission of the absolute, and when that great day comes it will be seen that a classical education was worth every penny that our parents paid for it. The Pythagoreans used form in the service of number, and it is obvious to me that the curve of your breast is a scientific approach to the infinity of bliss.'

ERIC LINKLATER, *A Terrible Freedom*

Rae and I were doing the dishes, she washing, me drying,
Looking out of our window over the road to the trees
At the edge of the park, and I saw a woodpigeon fly
Over and up and into the branches. 'I know what it is,'
I said. And Rae said, 'What?' And I said, 'The answer.
The answer to the riddle of the universe. Life, death,
And everything.' So we carried on doing the dishes.
It took a few minutes before Rae said, 'So it's not 42?'
So I said, 'No.' She waited another few minutes before,
With a sigh, she said, 'Well, what is it?' And I said,
'The shape of a curve.' And she said, 'So that's the answer?
That's it?' And I said, 'Aye. That's what it is.'
      And a few days later I was working in the office,
And Ken called in and asked me about Burns.
'The poet?' I said. 'Aye. What makes him so great?
Answer on postcard. Speak into microphone.
In a single sentence. Please answer now.'
      'His response to the shape of a curve,' I said.
For a few moments, we both stopped.
And then Professor Simpson said, 'That's it.'

The Return of the Great Auk

Not long after the Kelvingrove Museum reopened,
A friend phoned up, visiting Glasgow; I told him:
'Let's meet at the glass case with the Great Auk in it.'
'No,' he said, 'Too risky. Let's meet underneath the organ.'
So we did, but I went over to ask a long-faced attendant:
Where it would be? And the long face fell. The eyes
Became baleful. 'I'm awfy sorry sir,' he said —
'The number of folk who've asked me that...'
He sadly shook his head. 'Don't tell me,' I said,
'You haven't brought it up from the basement yet...'
He shook his head again. 'It's worse than that,
Sir,' he said. 'When we lifted it, it fell apart,
The feathers fell ti the flair. It just dis-
Intygrated. Turnt ti dust.' And so we left it there.
The last and final extinction of the Great Auk of Kelvingrove.

But a few years later, a few weeks ago,
I was there once again, with our youngest son,
Who wanted to visit the dinosaurs. Disconsolate and Aukless,
I turned a corner and saw it. In a glass case, clean, looking like
new. 'It's back!' I cried out. 'The Great Auk has returned!'
Life will find a way, I thought, as they say in *Jurassic Park*.
But I saw no sign of the long-faced attendant.

Driving home from Stratford

Anne Hathaway's cottage didn't do it for the boys.
Both were bored by wooden beams and mote-filled sunny air.
So let's go home. At last the border reaches us,
we roll the windows down for the sign: deep breaths and cries of,
'Scotland!' And then the rain starts. By Cumnock
it has all become torrential, vast, continuous: the four tyres
surf the tarmac, and the road as it crosses the high moors
suddenly is flecked by tiny chips of light, moving crosswise, jerkily,
in leaps and tiny jumps. 'What's that?' / 'What on earth are those?'
We don't slow down but we make them out: wee frogs.
An exodus of frogs, a mass migration, a gold-rush population shift,
from one field to another, across the whiplash winding road
and under the wheels of the car just now, and then, and now,
and there. We *won't* slow down and certainly don't swerve.
The boys for the first time that day, being little boys, twist round
and see the tiny corpses in the tail-lights, squished.
Then forward in the headlights, to watch. 'Get that one, Daddy!'
'You missed him!' / 'You got him! You got that one, Daddy!'
Such dark Shakespearian sport keeps them awake,
alert, attentive, eager, as we near home.

Co-ordinate Points

A portrait of David Daiches

1   What it's for

Your father dies: the shield is gone.
The sky is thus enlarged.
But the distances!
            The plenitude arrives
selectively, by family, and friends, and chosen
simply from the things of the world
if you are honest, to find
the shape of a curve —
the feelings to be honest to —

2   Sunny Day

Once more into the gated garden stepped
the couple in their age and with them then and there,
a younger couple and their son.
The sunlight through the leaves and branches spangled like a river
reflecting on a wooden wall in some tall airy staff room, say
in Cambridge, full of friendship, colleagues, plots.
The light was filtered, fine and clarified
the conversation, gestures, acts of arms and hands,
protecting the child, prospective.

3   *The Consolations of Scholarship*

So that when you come to the seat by the window,
lucky enough to have reached it,
the patience will help you sustain
the richness and values, the worth
of it all, the music, the scent
in the air, the taste of the earth.

4   *The piano*

Fingers on the keys
as our young son sits balanced on your knees
and reaches out his hands between your hands
and the melody you play
he begins to hear, and speak and say.

5   *The library*

The ladder to the books
moves sideways, you
climb up and down, our looks
follow that progress, keen,
without saying anything.
We both know what they mean.

6   In the Caledonian Hotel

'If you come upstairs, your table will be ready.'
The waitress had gone before she could have seen
your face already smiling at
the multiple strangeness of that: 'If we don't go upstairs,
will it *not* be ready? And how could she know
that it *will* be, not
that it already *is*?' The momentary
pleasure of it privilege allows, that vulnerable,
almost-nonsense thing, savoured, saved.

7   The interview at St Andrews

'And if you were appointed,
what exactly would you do?'
Bright mind of desire,
Oh what would you do?

'Why, I'd make this the centre
the hub and the hold
of Scotland, our literature,
all to be told!'

'Oh dear, dear, dear, dear!
Dear boy, can't you see?
There are English girls taught here!
That must never be!'

8   *The things that really matter*

The way Mozart predicts Mahler. Bartók's second
violin concerto. Glenmorangie. Language and the difference
of language. What you hear between the Scots
      — *Ye are na Mary Morison*
      and the English version of it.
'Chris once said he thought it was the best line Burns ever wrote.
That's why. In two small words there, everything is changed.
It is another language. All the difference in the world.'

9   *Free, but not directionless*

With songs to sing at daybreak
for the morning still to come!
To fill the night with laughter,
conversation's rivers,
thought and form and fortitude
in this unhurtful time.
Let's touch again the crockery and crystal,
the heavy-handled cutlery
and drape the napkin as you would in time,
that moves at the pace of the Pullman,
as it comes in under the ragged rise
of Edinburgh Castle's rock,
its angles unpredicted, purposeful,
like academic freedom and discussions we once had.

The Guy Rope

for Angus Calder, 1942–2008

'We carry in our worlds that flourish
our worlds that have failed,' wrote Christopher Okigbo, and you
would place that on the first clean page you had
before embarking on the journey to fill a thousand more of them,
telling all the stories of the worlds you could describe,
of people of all kinds, of 'the English-speaking Empires'
across three hundred years.

As a small boy takes his father's hand
and walks up the curved stone steps to the door
and goes into the church as the rain begins
and the guy rope that holds down the tent is taut as a bowstring –
each sentence in that book is well-mannered as that boy,
as tense as that string.

You remember that TV series *Porridge*?
When the old lag's time is up, he gives Ronnie Barker the boat
he spent the last twenty-five years building from matchsticks,
matchstick by matchstick. 'I don't want to take it wiv me,'
he explains. 'It's my life in 'ere, that is. Took me all me time
to do that. All me time.' And Ronnie looks at it and says,
'Was it worf it?'

And I'm reading the books you've written
And the poems and essays that say, Scotland:
Counter-argument: yes we can.

And I'm thinking of the work we did together,
of wind billowing white lace curtains in a room filled with books
and that big Pacific light, in the early morning of New Zealand,
and of dark Edinburgh nights, the walk from the deep enclosures of
The National Library of Scotland, down the long hill to your flat,
and I'm saying yes, it was worth it.
It is hard-won, the independent mind.
The outlaw status poetry insists upon.
I wouldn't want it any other way.

Tait's MacDiarmid

Piano notes, forthright, and chords, both bold and curious,
then song, a voice, a Scots voice, opening the air.
And in the air also, there is The Voice of the BBC
on radio waves, the information, official and approved —
(the books of poems, information, unofficial, the wedge) —
a radio, newspapers, poems and songs: What might you do,
   unorthodox,
against time and within it, measured and spontaneous, delicate
   and strong?

The vision moves along the clocks where they sit on the
   mantlepiece,
as their long and short hands move, around, then the vision
   moves
back along the other way, and it slows you down to see that:
time moving, the fire burning in the hearth, the grate,
the pot plants growing in their earth containments.

A man on the edge of a pavement,
on the rim of the squared slabs, balancing between
the raised stone platform by the road and
all its passing traffic, then stepping up and
walking on a wall, or down some stone steps,
down to the edge of the sea, by the rippling waves,
the dark encroaching waters of the sea, the man
throwing stones into the sea —

A glimmer of laughter, a ripple of his shoulders,
neck down, head dipped, a dodge, a piece of cheek
or mischief, disguising an accomplishment unspoken.

The door to the house opens.
He goes in. The door closes.
The thick carved wooden knocker is there
on the outside of the closed door.
The light goes on through the window,
the curtains are open — there is the unseen,
there is the invitation of the visible —
The multitude of books, inside!
The film by which we see them.

Melville in Glasgow

Consider it a sketch: charcoal on grain, white paper, black ash,
clouds and the Necropolis, the perfect size and shape of that
    Cathedral,
to see it from the south side of the Clyde and think of modesty
    and reach,
the country all around; to think of what was there, and what
that man was looking for, a past that might say more than all
    the risk
he'd known before he stepped up on that quay: what did he
    want?
A family? A line? A net? A country? A link in a chain he couldn't
    put down,
to haul up something far too deeply rusted out of sight; yet not
    too far:
he knew it was there, went looking for it, crossed the country,
    walked and rode and
came back in to Glasgow: his place, his port. The first and last he
    saw, of some-
thing then he must have thought ancestral, real as all the things
    he knew had happened
to him, in the South Pacific, visceral, in blood and muscle,
    yielding to delight,
yet also always fictional: build on that. On what? Where was
    he then?
What strength and what uncertainty, and what desire to know,
    dared push that pen?

Lanarkshire, January

low sun —
        late winter afternoon —
the shadows stroll and stretch themselves across
                        the green fields and the iron earth —
the widescreen light is cold and clarifies on paths white with frost,
all the lengthening day,
        from Loudon Hill to Tinto
from Darvel to Drumclog.

The spires of village churches
sharpen themselves, in the air.
Branches click like blades
or needles in the breeze.

Covenanter land: a hard terrain
of outdoor congregations, sheer
determination, beliefs
you'd stand and die with, live for in
commitment, be determined by.

                The bare trees
strain the sunlight in the sky.

The Dogs of Scotland

You only cross this border once —

The rain pulls back its curtain once again, and light
falls like sheaves from the clouds, harvests across
the horizon, stooked in the earth, leaning into sky.
The rain twists off like helter-skelter figures of eight,
fluent and returning all the time,
and the light says hello to the call
of all the dogs of Scotland,
opening their throats to the air.

You can hear them bark in sunshine in the city parks,
while foxes nose through bins in Glasgow alleys,
brazen on the edge of their domain, on borderlands.
While David, three years old, is running in the snowfall, all
   hands up
to an unending number of tiny wet kisses, now, for the first
   time only,
blessings in the country and the city, in an air too filthy and
   too clean
to want any more or less of, yet, so doggedly —
except this particular 'piece of the planet' forever.

February Morning: Traffic

for Chan Ky-Yut

The arc of the rim of the sun comes up
Above the farthest line, the nearest mist —

The sky is not more various, the sea
less careless of constraint
than all the Autumn golds of Canada,
the sharpest scattered reds along
the Old Silk Road you walk with —
the rising sun behind you —
your shadow leans ahead —
into the colours the winds make, the forms clouds'
shadows move upon.

The heron on the twisted branch
rising from the mud beneath
the flat stream by the back fields near
the houses on the edges of the city,
cranes its neck around, eyeing for gleids,
glimmers on the surface, ripples
over the movement
of wee fish underneath,
as the bus goes by on the motorway.

— From Ayr to Glasgow, green to grey,
the traffic curls and curves away
crowded, in flightpaths, like birds in endless patterns in the sky
moving in folds and lines and currents, sweeping it all away,
the grime in the air, the soot and charcoal blacks are washed
to the borders of the visible: river, backyards, buildings,
city, mountains, this horizon's rim
and still you can see it, see, even now,
'that old loveliness of earth that both affirms and heals'

Bus Stop, Alloway: Spring

The clouds are bigger than the hills.
The hills are known green, benign, walkable.
The trees on the skyline shapely, leaning
Gently. What takes us through distance
And days? What changes the past?
The acts and words, the scratching of
The green leaves in the trees above,
That tentative squirrel, nervously crossing the road,
The fragrance of wild garlic in the air,
For thirty seconds, then, that unpredicted burst of hail.

Drumelzier

I have to try to make some sense
of this strange place. It is as if translation
had been made, in language I can't emulate
or describe; but remember it
like this:
                I pulled the van over, on the gravel
by the sideroad, switched off the engine;
Jim and I got out. The sudden interruption
of movement, machine, the sharp metallic
edge of the van-doors shutting, key grating the lock,
released us into sunlight, afternoon, a loose but close assembly
of trees, leaves silver, green and whispering. The breeze was shifting
through them in directions, unpredicted. It was warm.
We walked across the road, down a yellow grass bank
to the flat triangle of field, beside the Powsail burn,
running there beside us towards the Tweed, which
we couldn't see, lower in a cut in the valley
ahead of us, where we could see the shadow
and the dark walls of trees beyond, on
the other side of the river.
                Shadows seemed to move among the leaves
and slowly, the perceptible audible context
was changed. We could hear
no more the rustling sound of leaves; we could hear
instead, an actual conversation, taking place.
You know how it is when your mind's half-focused,
your ears and eyes in a crowd and

what you hear and what you see are indistinct,
but certain, present, there? This was
like that. An actual conversation, voices, more
than two, a crowd, as if,
a party, talking, murmuring too low
to hear exactly what or what
their speech was of. Unobtrusive, unbelievable,
we looked around, and then at each other:
'Can you hear — '
                    'Aye...'
A silent smile; another. No
explanation possible, then or now. No-one else nearby
at all, for miles. We waited in the middle of the voices
as they spoke (not to us exactly; for us?
Certainly, we overheard or heard what was
within their world, as it was ours), then turned and
walked away from there.
                    More than twenty years,
from then to this. Maybe I decided
long ago, there are some things
no answers help.
                    I've heard of fearful
ghosts, but this was something warming, good,
a kind of shared acknowledgement, unexplained, a strange
translation, a mass of living language from beyond
whatever it was we could see, so clearly.

Crepusculario

In darkness how they haunt us, these shadows of a past we know —
a past we always know we're on the point of superseding —
always in the moment of the dawn's anticipation, letting go
of an evening spent before this sun had risen.

May all the hauntings be of favoured memories of real things
Not things you'd wish forgotten or that never should have happened.

Let them linger in their traces as they go. Let them lead to this.

The Bridge to Dunskiath

And this is the way the bridge was: the two ends of it
were low, and the middle was high...
LADY GREGORY, *Cuchulain of Muirthemne*

Approaching on the road from Tarskavaig,
you can see its arc, reaching
from the main island in a curve, up, over
and down to the rocky promontory. But when you walk
across the field to where it begins, you see that the bridge
is not there, only the stone of its arches and broken walls
on either side, reach over.
                              So to cross, it's your fingertips
and feet, your toes through your socks and shoes that grip
the small ledge beneath you, the crevice for handholds
over your head. The stone is secure but the crossing seems
perilous. Bad enough for us, but for our youngest boy, then nine,
once across, the worry stayed on his face about how to get back,
till he did. Climbing up the hewn steps in the stone
to the thick-grassed top of the rock, we all were getting higher,
deeper in. The ocean broke from slate to white around us, roaring.

Here the young Cuchulain met the woman Skathach,
who taught him the arts of war. And this was where
her sunny house was, with its seven great doors
and seven great windows between every two doors
and couches between the windows
and beautiful young women
with scarlet cloaks and blue clothes on them, waiting for him.

And this was where Cuchulain loved
and bred with Skathach's daughter
and from this place his child would follow him
sworn by his vengeful mother to silence
until his father, in the midst of slaughter, learned
that this was his own son he'd wounded mortally,
upon the point of dying.

Cuchulain then determined to fight death
and walked into the sea to close with it.

We stood upon the rock of Skathach's castle,
surrounded by the cliffs and ocean breaking,
having crossed to that place, pausing to wonder
before trying to find our way back.

Some other books published by **LUATH** PRESS

Arts of Resistance: Poets, Portraits and Landscapes of Modern Scotland

By Alan Riach and Alexander Moffat, with contributions by Linda MacDonald-Lewis
ISBN 1 906817 18 9 PBK £16.99

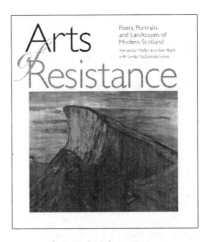

The role of art in the modern world is to challenge and provoke, to resist stagnation and to question complacency. All art, whether poetry, painting or prose, represents and interprets the world. Its purpose is to bring new perspectives to what life can be.

ALEXANDER MOFFAT and ALAN RIACH

arts *n* (1) any imaginative or creative narrative, or non-scientific branch of knowledge eg. literature, history, fine art, music; (2) ingenious abilities or schemes

resistance *n* (1) standing firm, refusing to submit; (2) a covert organisation fighting for national liberty in a country under enemy occupation.

There will always be a need for the arts to provide forms of resistance to any thing that dulls or numbs the intellect or the sensual understanding of the world. The artists and writers of the 20th century had to contend with an era characterised by rapid change in perspectives and technology, and the political force of their work informed, abraded and catalysed their contemporaries. In the 21st century, we live in an age of distraction. The arts are the greatest force for the best that people can do, and we neglect them at our peril. Arguing that to be truly international, you have to be national to begin with, the authors look at the power of nationhood to create roots from which art can grow. Challenging the view that there is no Scottish art, they debate the contribution of poets, artists and others from the late 19th century to the present day, including William McTaggart, Hugh MacDiarmid, the Scottish Colourists and Charles Rennie Mackintosh.

Beyond the Sun: Scotland's Favourite Paintings

Poems by Edwin Morgan

ISBN 1 905222 72 6 HBK £9.99

For years Scotland has nurtured the relationship between literature and art. Indeed, many of Scotland's finest writers began their careers at art school – Alasdair Gray, John Byrne and Liz Lochhead, amongst others. It is a connection to cherish. *Beyond the Sun* adds a further dimension to this flowering relationship between poetry and painting.

In September 2005, readers of *The Herald* newspaper voted for their ten favourite paintings in Scotland. Topping the list was the stunning Salvador Dali's 'Christ of St John of the Cross', but also included were poignant classics such as Avril Paton's 'Windows in the West' and Sir Henry Raeburn's 'Reverend Robert Walker Skating on Duddingston Loch'. Edwin Morgan, Scotland's most popular poet, was so fascinated and inspired by these paintings that he immediately penned a poem to honour each one, and sent the handwritten originals to Lesley Duncan, poetry editor at *The Herald*. These poems perfectly complement the paintings and the result is a moving collection which comes at a time when Scotland is yet again defining its cultural status in the world with the re-opening of Kelvingrove Art Gallery and Museum. The book begins with introductory essays by Lesley Duncan and Alan Riach, Professor of Scottish Literature at Glasgow University, and ends with a touching afterword by Glasgow's Poet Laureate, Liz Lochhead.

100 Favourite Scottish Love Poems

Edited by Stewart Conn

ISBN 1 906307 66 0 PBK £7.99

Poems of passion. Poems of compassion. Poems of cherishing. Poems of yearning. Poems that celebrate and illuminate. Poems vibrant with the tenderness and heartbreak of love.

Embracing love reciprocated and love unrequited, this selection ranges from irrepressible optimism to longing and loss; from lovers' abandon to parental affection. There are poems for every lover and loved one to savour and share, and to touch the heart. But leaving plenty room for humour and a whiff of sour grapes.

Stewart Conn mines Scotland's rich seam of love poetry in its different tongues – from traditional ballads, Burns and Scott to MacCaig, MacLean, Morgan and the vitality of Liz Lochhead and Jackie Kay; from 'Barbara Allan', 'The Blythesome Bridal' and 'Lassie Lie Near Me' to 'Hot Chick', 'Yeah Yeah Yeah' and 'Out with my Loves on a Windy Day'.

Wallace Muse: poems inspired by the life & legacy of William Wallace

Edited by Lesley Duncan/Elspeth King
ISBN 1 905222 29 7 PBK £8.99

The power of Wallace
Cuts through art
But art calls attention to it
Badly or well

from *Lines for Wallace* by Edwin Morgan

Sir William Wallace – bloodthirsty and battle-hardened hero, liberator and creator of Scotland. Wallace the man was a complex character – loved by the Scots, loathed by the English, a terror to some, an inspirational leader to others. No matter what side you are on, William Wallace is an unmistakable and unforgettable historical figure whose actions at the Battle of Stirling Bridge helped free the Scottish nation. The life and legend of Wallace has been a Muse providing inspiration to poets and artists from Scotland and across the globe for 700 years. From great epic to McGonagall, the violent to the poignant, this collection highlights the impact that the memory of Wallace has made on the nation's culture for centuries.

Life Sentence: More Poems Chiefly in the Scots Language

By Rab Wilson
ISBN 1 906307 89 X PBK £8.99

We haud the universe
athin oor grup,
Syne life cams pourin frae
the biro's tip,
An thon primordial urge
we hae tae tell,
Come spillin oot, frae
whaur? Nae man can tell –
Fir Life is whit we aa are sentenced tae.

Rab Wilson can find poetry everywhere in life; in a shopping trolley in the river, a trip to the bookie's, or a catastrophic earthquake. In this lichtsome new collection, he digs into literature ('Where Burns Has Wrote, In Rhyming Blether...'), history ('Rab Bruce, Drug Baron, Addresses his Troops'), terrorism ('Israeli Bombs at Prestwick') and social commentary ('Misanthrope in the Pound-Shoap').

Written in Scots and English, the language of the poems is versatile and expressive, adding texture, comedy or earthiness to everyday events. When taking a sly poke at other people's pretensions or reflecting on world peace, Rab's 'Life Sentence' never weighs too heavily on his shoulders.

Details of these and other books published by Luath Press can be found at:
www.luath.co.uk

Luath Press Limited
committed to publishing well written books worth reading

LUATH PRESS takes its name from Robert Burns, whose little collie Luath (*Gael.*, swift or nimble) tripped up Jean Armour at a wedding and gave him the chance to speak to the woman who was to be his wife and the abiding love of his life. Burns called one of 'The Twa Dogs' Luath after Cuchullin's hunting dog in Ossian's *Fingal*. Luath Press was established in 1981 in the heart of Burns country, and is now based a few steps up the road from Burns' first lodgings on Edinburgh's Royal Mile.

Luath offers you distinctive writing with a hint of unexpected pleasures.

Most bookshops in the UK, the US, Canada, Australia, New Zealand and parts of Europe either carry our books in stock or can order them for you. To order direct from us, please send a £sterling cheque, postal order, international money order or your credit card details (number, address of cardholder and expiry date) to us at the address below. Please add post and packing as follows: UK – £1.00 per delivery address; overseas surface mail – £2.50 per delivery address; overseas air-mail – £3.50 for the first book to each delivery address, plus £1.00 for each additional book by airmail to the same address. If your order is a gift, we will happily enclose your card or message at no extra charge.

Luath Press Limited
543/2 Castlehill
The Royal Mile
Edinburgh EH1 2ND
Scotland
Telephone: 0131 225 4326 (24 hours)
Fax: 0131 225 4324
email: sales@luath.co.uk
Website: www.luath.co.uk